THE
MAGICIAN

PATRIK J. BAUDIN

Ordering Information:

Prime Seven Media
518 Landmann St.
Tomah City, WI 54660

Printed in the United States of America

Introduction

If you want to know life, study death, and if you want to know death, study life.

To begin with, I would like to warn you against performing this form of magic. If you are not psychologically stable and do not treat this magical path with deep respect and honour, you could very well be led into insanity or even worse.

I also want to make it clear that I will always recommend everyone to follow their doctors advice, instead of solemnly relying on magical operations to treat either physical or mental illnesses.

It is true, according to my own experiences that magical procedures can certainly manifest miracles around the operator, but it is also true that the same can emphasize or even manifest new and worse problems than what you used the procedure to change in the first place. It is therefore very important to know yourself and your limits very well before you dive into the unknown seas of the occult principles of magical operations in practice. Magic is, at its best, an unstable science and the magicians path is about stabilizing that rocky path into something useful and understandable.

To be a magician, is to be a constant seeker of wisdom and evolution of your own reality in order to prepare the way for others to pass through the heavy gates of their own development and self awareness. It is to live through the legends of Prometheus in a symbolical sense. To understand the fight that Enki had for mankind, and the true meaning of Gilgamesh journey into the underworld of his own subconciouss.

A magician is someone that covets the apples of Idunn, not only for himself, but also for the noble brothers and sisters of this magical and astounding creation that we share with each other, weather we want it, or not.

Considering the magicians personal journey, the magical procedure is in itself very closely connected to modern psychotherapy.

The way towards enlightment is to enlighten the darkerst corners of your own subconciouss. When you know yourself, you will find a way to the collective subconciouss.

The body of the collective subconciouss can be seen upon as a dimension, or realm in itself. Some may draw parallels to the first ethers that esoteric teachings have described through symbolism since the dawn of mankind. And I find those parallels very close to my own reality. How I perceive myself and the creation I currently inhabit.

Before you embark upon this journey into unknown waters, it is very important to have in mind that the collective subconciouss is just a doorstep into higher realms. It is one of the ways towards the mountain top and not the only one.

It is one of the means to travel towards your own subconcioussness, and through that towards the collective subconscious, beyond witch lies full enlightenment, a revelation of your own being and existence.

Even Carl Gustaf Jung admitted that some of the beings that he conjured up through his subconciouss had their own personality and self awareness. The question, for him, was more if these beings were the creation of the collective archetyphical symbolism manifested, or if they were a creation of itself, roaming the collective subconscious of mankind.

The modus operandi of his research reminds me of a magicians path in many ways. So it is easy for me to see his lifelong journey to find these answers. However, as I see it, the journey is more important than the destination in these matters.

According to experience through years of experimentation I have formed my own opinion that what Jung describes as the collective subconciouss, is to be seen upon as a dimension that all dimensions and beings in this creation is bound to and from. In it, we can find entities created by other beings connected, as well as beings from other dimensions and realms that roams it and in some cases exist only there instead of were they are from. It is a portal to any place or time in the creation itself.

Anyone can, with a bit of effort create a living being with a personality of its own that will inhabit the collective realm, fully capable of affecting the surrounding realms. The higher energy, or frequency that your soul vibrates in, the more you can affect other members of the collective.

Magical evocation is a way to raise your energy and to train your abilities in this methodology.

A well trained magician can certainly affect feelings and emotions of a nation, and in rare cases whole worlds. His feelings and intentions are felt by all that are connected to this collective body.

As a magician, you have to apply reason to your experiences. Otherwise you would be lost in theoretical illusions that will form and manifest your own realities. Empirical philosophy must cooperate with practical philosophy to form a common ground, a neutral field of exploration for your own personal synthesis and theorems. Do not limit yourself unto empirical facts. Instead, try to understand the basis of it. Why is it manifesting in this or that way.

To understand the realities of other realms, you can not use the natural laws of your own realm as a foundation. The higher you climb upon the mountain top, the more you will have to shift your view upon its foundation.

You must study and understand the cause before you can theorize about its effects. This is where the symbolism of "Jacobs ladder" can be understood in its full extent. The stairway to heaven is manifested through your conscious acts of will to understand and manifest what you desire without a personal ego. Some things are not to be said, but to be understood. And this is also why we have the mystery schools of antiquity and some of the lodges of our modern society.

The journey itself will influence the nature of its destination. Each and every man and woman is a star, meaning that we all create and manifest our own reality. When God created man, he did it in his own image. We are all our own Gods and Goddesses, never forget that, and never use that to try to become someone elses God or Goddess. If you do that, remember that it is one of the key elements that forms your spiritual psychosis that leads towards your own insanity and misfortune. It will destroy you and your personal reality. And this is why it is the forbidden fruit from the tree of knowledge. If you eat it, you will most probably missuse its effects in such a degree that it will destroy you. The knowledge itself will expel you from your comfort zone, the rest of mankind. Instead of working with you, the beings that you conjure up, will work against you. You will be an outcast of the spiritual and physical community.

Everyone who finds positive experiences of magical manifestations that can be personally verified and documented without any dault, will be very affected both psychologically as well as physically. The world will never be the same after such, both in a negative and a positive way.

One of the hardest obstacles in the successful magicians path is actually the isolation from the so called real world. People around you have no idea what you have experienced, and will never understand what you are trying to describe from your point of view after being shown the other realities that surrounds this creation and an infinity of others.

Wisdom is as rare, as it is dangerous, and just as in the dark ages witch processes you will at best be judged as dabbeling with something dark and forbidden, or as in most cases in this current society, as a dillusional lunatic ready for psychotherapy.

Remember that it is not that long time ago when enlightened people like Nicolaus Copernicus, Galileo Galilei and Leonardo Da Vinci where considered to be completely lunatics by the established scientific community at the time. Today we celebrate these universal geniouses as brilliant instead of insane. The image of the world has changed, but the behavior of mankind stays on a firm path. Be a member of the pack, or you will be an outcast.

The moment that you decide to become an operative magician, you also have to accept being an outcast.

It is also in context to remember that some nations still burn people with a different view upon spirituality and interdimensional exploration than what they, themselves have, at the stake.

When you look at the current pioneers of the scientific community like for example within quantum mechanics and astrophysics, it is hard to understand how people can overlook what science actually implies. But the explanation is as simple as it is sad. Very few humans of today keep up to date with the latest news from multiple sciences, no matter how overwhelming and fantastic results that are published. If you are not a scientist yourself, you will most probably not read those articles, and certainly not understand them.

If you actually are a scientist, in one form or another, you will most certainly not connect it with the ancient wisdom of magical and alchemical operations. You would look upon earlier magical explorers as superstitious and dumb.

My advice is that you should always explore the unknown without perceptual filters to distort your reality. You do this for yourself, so don't lie to yourself. Always see upon your experiences as a newborn would look upon the world around it. Be positive to manifest positive results.

Without respect and understanding of not only the ritual modus operandi, its symbolism, and the entities it involves, the sling shot effects will destroy your life as you know it right now. To begin with, everything that could go wrong goes wrong. Then your health will be affected severely, you will become seriously ill. After this your economy will be cast into ruins. Your friends and loved ones will distance themselves from you. Nightmares and deep depressions will haunt you constantly, and insanity will carefully lure you into a deep and dark abyss without return.

However, if you treat the magical operations with deep respect and honor, and perform it with a good intention in order to evolve yourself spiritually into becoming better than yourself. If you perform it in order to improve your own, and/or your loved ones life, you will experience positive results without the so called sling shot effects.

If you have this in mind, you can use this form of magic to evolve beyond your current comprehension of yourself and your understanding of the multiverse. You can be a pioneer that explores the furthest borders of human evolution and boldly go where few have gone before.

If you start to experience negative effects, keep in mind that you manifest most of it yourself. Always have possible slingshot effects and negative results in mind, so that you don't let your own paranoia enforce it.

It is my recommendation that you have at least some form of experience within ritual high magic, spiritual workings or other experiences from conjuration of spiritual entities before you embark on this quest. Don't perform these rituals out of curiosity of the occult, do it out of curiosity about yourself and your place in the creation. Look at these experiments as a process of self development, and later as a means to empower and improve the lives of not only yourself but also your loved ones. The rewards are many for a serious magician with a good intention.

Many magicians in the history of mankind have argued about the reality of the beings that they conjured up. Are they real; or, are they just the result of a psychological phenomenon driven forth by a state of deep trance that activates parts of your brain that you usually don't use? Are they archetypical representations of your subconscious mind, or are they beings with a personality of their own?

My own conclusion, after nearly a lifetime of careful experimentation with not only the Goetic spirits but also with most of the known grimoires of today, is that they are all right. Psychology has always been close at heart in my studies and personal development, just as history, philosophy and archaeology have helped me to form the path upon which I'm currently walking. I would rather say that I know, instead of belive.

The beings recorded in the Goetic texts can be real beings with a personality of their own, fully capable of producing external phenomena that can not be explained through ordinary scientific models.

If you look upon them in this way when conjuring them, they will also appear in that way.

However, if you treat them as just another psychological phenomena, they would, for sure, appear as such.

In order to get into contact and work with the original 72 beings of the Goetia, you must also be convinced of their existence. If you do not have that conviction, different parts of your brain will produce a phenomena according to your own perceptual filters. Or you might just evoke the egregoire type of entities that you find in various lodges and magical communities of today. Considering that almost all soccer fan clubs and role playing societies, lodges, churches, religions and similar gatherings have an egregoire that could easily be mistaken for one of the 72 angels of King Salomon, its easy to get a comprehension of what could go wrong when conjuring the real entities of this interesting grammar.

The first time I read about Carl Gustav Jung's theories concerning archetypes and symbolism, I felt that he was very close to the truth of the human consciousness in religion and to the very essence of philosophical thinking. His theories about the collective subconscious and archetyphical images were the first step towards a slight understanding of spirituality and the spiritual beings that surrounded me in constant manifistations. But above that it had to be more hiding behind the scene.

I had at that time constant experiences of spiritual beings in full physical manifestations all around me. My dreams and visions about future events always unfolded step by step, most often already the day after I had received hem, and sometimes years after its appearance to me. The visions were never as easy and basic as simple déjà vu experiences. They were always complicated descriptions of coming events. Actually, visions about coming events were as frequent as visions about the past and present time. If someone hid something from me, I just asked where it was before I went to bed, and then I would find the answer through the collective subconscious during my sleep. The day after, I would know exactly where to look.

Some of the entities were so physical in their manifestations that I thought they were real life humanlike beings. Until I found out what they were, these manifestations usually scared the hell out of me as they started to manifest and present themselves at a very young age. The "moving stars" and light manifistations were a constant and secret companion to me. And they have been already from my first memories when I began to observe them. I looked upon them as naturally as I would look upon the rest of the world around me.

When I was about eleven-years old, they started to guide me into making my first Seals of Solomon on small brass plates that I found in a container in an industrial area near my home. At the same time, I also started to develop high levels of telekinesis and mind reading techniques. Early on, I had to do everything in secret and I only had negative responses from the few friends that I showed what I was capable of doing. Due to this negativity, I lost interest and did my very best to deny what was all around and within me.

I refused to follow the guidance I received about things that others didn't consider natural and common in life. My hardest task at that time in my life was to fit in, and to appear as normal as my surroundings appeared. What I knew and experienced became more of a curse than a blessing for a long time. I hated to feel so different and did my very best to deny myself and my destiny as a magician and a conjurer. What others considered supernatural, I considered as natural as brushing your teeth in the morning. But what others considered natural, seemed to me as unnatural as going naked to school.

The path of a magician is a hard one to follow, and it is filled with tests that will make you hate yourself and your destiny more than anyone outside of it can ever comprehend. I found it useful to become informed about the world around me in my quest as a magician. Accuracy and application of what was written in the text books and literature were not always straightforward and in these instances, I could get confirmation from the entities that were surrounding me.

Archaeology and history often became a personal conflict for me, as what I remembered from past incarnations rarely agreed with the world of academics. What we see today in books about the past, is usually the result of a strong influence from rulers and religious authorities in the past. The theories of archaeology are most often formed by academics that build castles out of grains of sand. It has become more important with academic status and reputation, than common sense and wisdom.

However, I very much enjoyed studying and practicing archaeology, even though I had to adapt into my academic environment and be careful of what I presented in my reports. After a few years of practice, studies, and a nice scholarship to a foreign university, I took a job as a night watch at an old cemetery. It was at this time where the light manifestations around me increased significantly in frequency and I realized that it was time for me to embrace my fate in full.

The more I looked the other way, the more intense the physical manifestations of extra dimensional beings around me became. During the first couple of years, I had about 40 to 50 full physical manifestations visiting me during my rounds each night. The point of no return came when other persons around me started to see and experience the visitations. I could hardly go outside during daytime, when the streets were filled with people, as they kept on coming, no matter where or when it was.

It became harder and harder for me to keep my secret from others. And, as I worked with high level security, I was always surrounded by cameras and other people. Here, I must give my deepest of respect and gratitude towards especially one colleague that kept my secret when he started to see and experience the manifestations around me. It is very rare to meet such a wise and old spirit incarnated in your surroundings today. Without his friendship and careful support, I would have given up my destiny very early.

My guides started by stearing me into the old systems of magic. As I already knew, the world is not what it seems through the eyes of today's media and science. So the first step was to isolate myself as much as possible. I turned off the TV, and stopped reading anything that wasn't about magic or philosophy. I stayed inside of my 100 square-meter apartment in the center of Copenhagen. All that mattered was my learning. As I worked in twelve hour shifts three nights a week, I rarely went outside during daylight. All my meals were consumed after sunset, before my 10 to 12 hour rites began each night that I was not working at the cemetery. I lived in complete chastity, with no contact to the outside world, except from sporadic contact with the closest family.

During a few years, all that mattered for me, was my studies of all the grimoires that I could find. I spent more time within the circle of power than what I did outside of it. Magic became a lifestyle and not just an interest, or a search for any particular answers.

After mastering many different conjuring technics, I started to perfect them with experiments upon willing people from all over the world through social media on the internet. I carefully documented and developed the technics of the experiments. During the most intense period I conjured, for free, for 20 to 30 different individuals four nights every week.

Few of them realized what I did, and to what extent I was doing it. And here I must appologize to all of those that were driven into a spiritual psychosis from the effects of my magic. The purpose and intent has always been, and still is, to spread the joy and love of the wonders that I, myself, have experienced through contact with higher dimensional beings. The magic was intended to find a way to help others into a higher state of conscious, as fast as possible. with as little negative effects as possible.

Nothing can be compared to the first time that you stand in front of a huge golden light orb that comes down from the stars to the ground right in front of you when you call upon them.

Your whole world will be turned upside down in an instant. It will be as someone rips the carpet from the ground that your feet stand so securely upon.

You will start to question everything that you thought you knew about the world and science of today. Nothing will ever be the same again.

With this, you will also experience the paradox that Socrates spent a lifetime to investigate after the oracle at Delphi stated that he was the wisest man alive. The wiser you become, the less you know.

The higher you climb upon the mountain, the broader view you will have. And with a broader view, you will also have more to explore. One answer will only lead to another question in a never ending spiral of self exploration.

The reason to why I mention my own personal experiences here is to help those that have reached a higher level in their own development, and now experience the harsh tests that a magician is always confronted with. Trust me, things will look better when you give in to it, and start to do what your destiny has already written for you.

As I look upon my own development and path through the world of magic, I can see that I was carefully guided through many important steps that you can find in most of the old system magic. Feks the way that are described in"The sacred magic of Abramelin the mage" translated by S. Liddel MacGregor Mathers.

I had my so called forty days in the desert; it just became a longer journey than expected. I lived like ancient magicians before great workings, only in a form adapted into the more modern society. I ventured into the deepest and darkest corners of my own mind and personality for many years before i returned into the path of magical development and power.

As mentioned above, I even lived in chastity for a few years, and consumed all of my meals after sunset, usually vegetarian.

All that my mind was consuming was ancient grimoires, texts of philosophy and ancient wisdom. Most of my time was spent in the magic circle, conjuring higher beings, the rest of it roaming an old cemetery at nighttime.

This process was necessary to prepare me to"cross the abyss" as a few magicians call it.

If your intention is to reach the highest levels of magic, you must do your very best to follow the ancient advices about the neophytes path to high ceremonial magics.

This path can be divided into a few steps witch can be easily adapted into a modern lifestyle.

First you need to isolate yourself as much as possible. Only speak to the ones most necessary to speak to. Keep it to very close friends, relatives and work. Never speak about your experiments with others, no matter what miracles you manifest in your surroundings. It is your own journey, not theirs.

Second, avoid all forms of news and media. Close down your internet and only use it for absolutely necessary correspondence, and for finding information concerning your magic.

Third, if possible, intake all of your meals after the sun has set, and try to make those meals from something that is not dead. You don't have to become a complete vegetarian, but it helps if you keep it that way at least from the day before each great ritual.

Fourth, if you are not living in a close relation, try to live in chastity, or at least as close to it as possible.

Your mind should be clean, meaning that you must be focused solemnly on the great work, at least during your first experiments. Part of receiving the full support from the other realms is about showing your seriousness. You show that you are willing to sacrifice these parts of your life to find out the truth. That your mind is focused solemnly upon your own re integration.

The best is, if only you have access to the area designated as your temple, at least for the first six months of your practice. After that, your temple should be virtuous enough to repel all negative effects.

Fifth, avoid inviting people to your home, and especially into the area or room that you have consecrated into a temple. If a woman in her menstrual cycle enters your temple, it takes a month to make it pure again. Be careful about who you invite, people are unclean in many and various ways. Look upon your temple as a diplomatic ground.

One of the first great workings that all of this led me to was the conjuration of all of the 72 angels of the Goetia along with all of their servants, during the same rite, to swear their allegiance and support to me and my magics.

After this I continued my journey and did the same thing with the angels of the wind from "The Heptameron" by Peter de Abano, and many other beings from many other grimoires and magical systems that followed shortly after.

This has taught me, among other things that the meaning of magic power without wisdom is worth nothing.

The more powerful you become, the less you care about the actual power. And the more you can affect mankind with magic, the less you will use it. When you experience many and various miracles daily for a long time, you start to appreciate the lesser miracles in your everyday.

In the start of my training, I used to skim through the headlines of the major papers every day, and when I saw something that I did not like, I did my best to alter the situations with magic. I thought it was the right thing to do, as I could do it. Who else would be able to do such a thing? After all, the miracles I witnessed every day, is something that is very rare even for the most powerful of magicians.

After a couple of years like that, I realized that it leads to nothing, as the situations never changed permanently. Human nature dictates its fate more than any magic can affect it. It is what we usually refer to as the free will of mankind, or as I see upon it, the fall of mankind.

The best example of this is when I saw evil and malicious dictators killing their own people. I did my very best to curse them, haunt them, and even draw life force energy from them. In some cases I even threw powerful" death spells" upon them.

Shortly after, someone worse would enter the political scene in their nation. And I would in return, receive horrible negative backfiring effects that in some cases nearly killed me.

These experiments drew me into a long period were I started to doubt myself and my own intentions. Am I evil? Or am I doing a good thing for my fellow brothers and sisters of mankind.

Evil is a matter of perspective, and I am very sure that at least one of the dictators saw me as pure evil incarnated. At least that is what he said to me while cursing me with all the words that he knew from his own religious upbringing while I visited him astrally to draw his life-force from him.

I will never forget the last scenes of his life, broadcasted on CNN.

Another good example is when I had a very bad date. Earlier in the evening, she told me that she would be participating in a music festival outside. So I ordered a flooding of biblical proportions on that date, and in that place. It ended up with a horrific flooding that killed many of my dear cats that followed me around at the cemetery were I used to work during the graveyard shift at the time.

This example showed me that your magics affect many others. It is a long chain of events that will change the lives of many when used for a personal gain.

The memories of those kittens still haunt my dreams, and I regret doing it.

So, when I simplify, and adapt the ritual modus operandi, it is not out of some profane disrespect towards the ancient technics that I perfectly well know fulfill the purpose of the performance. It is because I want to offer a way into the world of magics and wonders to anyone that wants to explore it in today's modern society.

There are many paths towards the mountain top, and you are the one that walks upon it. Remember that. The most powerful magical system is the one that you develop yourself after much experience and failures. Training makes master.

So, when some self-proclaimed master claims that he knows the only way to the top, you should just smile and walk away. That master is not a master.

You should use others experiences and learn from them. But don't think that you will end up in the same place just because you use the same shoes as them.

No religion is the right religion, and all religion is the right religion.

"God created man in his own image, in the image of God he created him; male and female he created them." –Genesis 1:27

These famed words of the quote from Genesis are among the most known, and yet overlooked words from the foundation of many and various branches of religions. This simple sentence implies that there is a God and a Goddess, and that mankind, as their creation, was meant to be the same as them. It talks about equality and balance.

Religion is built by fear and control. The way to self-awareness is to face your fears and take control of the reality you live in.

Without contradictions there would be no religion. Religion is about dividing existence into good and bad, darkness and light, so that the simple human mind can understand itself and its own actions. It is a way to explain what you cannot explain. As a religious person you follow what others consider to be the truth and as a spiritual person, you find that truth yourself. The nature of human conciuous and the biology itself dictates a dual perspective upon its existence. The human psyche is divided into feminine and masculine thinking, anima and animus. And the brain itself consists of this duality in its right and left parts. One is rooted in your logical and aware activities, and the other in your subconscious mind. If we study religious and spiritual symbolism through history, it is very obvious how this manifests through dreams and visions of spiritual teachers exploring their subconscious reality.

In the dawn of mankind spiritual explorers saw upon darkness and light as a unity. One does not exist without the other. The polytheistic approach had members of the divine family that fought the same moral and ethical struggles as mankind did. They walked among humans as physical beings bound to this reality. The more monotheistic approach mankind took to their gods and goddesses, the more the divine distanced itself from human reality and entered their own. The male principle became the dominant force as God entered the world of the subconscious mind and stayed there.

It is very important to understand the difference between your personal as well as mankind's image of God, and what God actually is.

The image of God is formed by the human psyche and its struggles through history. This image is carefully nurtured by harsh events that cannot be understood without a higher purpose. God becomes an object of personal and cultural projections. This does not mean that you cannot find God, the subject, in religion.

The religious body is built of many components and the subjective God is the subconscious of that organism.

A primus motor in the evolution of mankind is to always overestimate its own importance individually as well as a collective. To find some form of understanding of the subjective God you must leave this ego behind and see yourself as a part of all things.

The enlightened man is aware of himself and have access to the gathered knowledge of the multiverse itself. He can see and feel through every stick and stone of the creation, with a simple thought. He is connected and self aware of the source energy we can call the subjective God. His divine spark is lit by the fire that

Prometheus stole from the Gods and gave to mankind. This fire illuminates the darkest corners of his own subconscious, he becomes illuminated, a part of the true illuminati.

By studying religion we learn more about ourselves than what we do of the subjective God. When we understand ourselves, we can study religion in a new perspective were we can comprehend the subjective God through the evolution of the human thought process.

To find this comprehension, we must study the whole man and not only parts. We cannot limit our search to psychology, philosophy, medicine, physics, history, archaeology, astronomy or any other science as a singularity. We must rise above the borders between faculties and look at the whole image.

Without the Devil, there would be no God. With a lack of concept for the most primeval darkness you cannot understand the brightest of light. Every successful superhero with good moral and ethical actions has an archenemy that do the opposite by performing actions that we all secretly dream of doing ourselves, hence the original sin.

These characters are easily found with a conjuration of them from the collective subconscious. Are they eternal beings that have always been there, or are they a creation/ manifestation of the collective itself? I would say both, as you can find them all through history by simply studying the pantheons and symbolism of religious mythos. They appear, were religious mythos appears. From time to time, they shift appearance and name to fit better into the populous conscious selves. As the gods seem to follow the conscious mind, wouldn't it then be fair to assume that they are the same? Gods are within the conscious mind, and they all exist within us all.

The symbolism of the mirror represents your logic, and just like a reflection upon the waters on a calm sea hides something deeper, so does your mind if you go past the surface and enter your subconscious.

A few texts of ancient Gnosticism describes this very clearly. They speak of a God that can be found in everything, and in everyone. Like for example the famed quote from the gospel of Thomas; "…split a rock and you will find me there."

God is a creative conscious energy that permeates all things in this creation. It is the self-awareness and primus motor of the multiverse itself. In other words, you are all connected to the great architect. No one have to follow the dictatorial steps of churches and religious institutions towards their image of what God should or should not be.

If you believe that your destiny leads to a fiery pit called hell, that is also were you will certainly end up when your conscious self leaves this dimension to enter others.

The collective subconscious is closely connected to what magicians and spiritual travelers call the astral realm. Through the astral realm, a well-trained traveller can easily affect the subconscious of anyone connected. He can even enter the dreams and visions of the subject and change it after thought and will, just as in the astral realms. This is also how a firm believer in a fiery pit, can create it after his own image in the astral realm. Through millennia's of focused will from millennia's of souls, this place became a reality in the astral realm. The fiercest demons of their imagination is also to be found there, just as evil as they thought it was.

Therefore, one man, can by telling a story about another reality, and gather many that put their faith and will into it, create such a place for us all. A kingdom of heaven and the fabled utopia appears through a subconscious manifestation into the astral realms.

The same metaphysical principal can be studied in the creation of a lodge egregoire, or in the making of a Golem entity by a skilled magician.

An advanced magician knows very well that what is manifested in the astral realm, can also be summoned into this physical dimension as a solid manifestation. As above so is below.

This theorem suggests a form of comprehension to an all knowing, omnipresent and omnipotent God. I say comprehension as full understanding is not possible when your mind is bound by the laws of nature in this reality.

God appears as a cognitive being that evolves through the evolution of the collective mind and spirit. Spirit becomes the conscious itself. Your soul is defined by your concuss self-awareness. However, this does not mean that what we consider non aware beings have no soul. Creative energy is the essence of the soul. As mentioned all things in this creation have this creative energy within. So, we can assume that all things and beings in this creation have a soul. And that we are all connected to each other through this bound.

In this sense we can also see the creation itself as one single body moving towards the same purpose. This means that if you harm someone, you also harm a part of yourself. We can with ease see this effect through the slingshot effects of all magic.

It is impossible to separate the essence of God from its creation. But it is my opinion that it is the collective mind and spirit that evolves with the evolution of God. Even though it is a contradiction to assume that something eternal and nonlinear can evolve in the sense that we put into the word evolve. It is even wrong to call God eternal, considering the word eternal is describing something that exists in the sphere of non-eternal and linear. Something that is bound by, and affected by time itself.

The creative energy permeates all dimensions and realms in this creation without any boundaries. It is therefore wrong to limit its essence by describing it as a cause of linear reality.

God is the cause and his creation the effect. But according to my own experiences the cause was present before the effect. So I would not limit God by saying that he would not be without his creation. I would not even say that he is in anyway dependent upon the existence of his own creation. The divine energy was formed by the creation it triggered. The creation itself is just what we perceive to be the reality and that is not necessarily the truth. Mankind is just in its infancy of self-discovery and many things will change as it evolves towards adulthood.

If you want to know the artist, you must study his art. In this case it means yourself, as well as your own surroundings. Know yourself, but do not assume that your reality is mine. Each and every man and woman is a star on its own path. So you must also have in mind that enlightment for you, is not necessarily the same for others. Neither is the way to reach it.

When you study the grand religions of this world, you can find many common traits that seems to permeate them all.

A good example of this is if you look at the Christ figure, and compare it with older perceptions of a godlike figure that represents his/ her family from heaven, or the stars. The entity of God, and his son, is a very powerful archetype that surfaces from the depths of our most primitive mind.

When I visited a cathedral in south France, dedicated to the black Madonna (Virgin Mary) last year, I started to receive visions from what I used to perceive as the mother goddess of the so called pagan cultures of the ancient days. This goddess was perceived as the dark Goddess, the Goddess of darkness and night, Artemis Diana, Diana Lucifera, Hecate and so on.

In fact, she has come to me in so many shapes that I can easily understand her connection throughout most of the religions in this world.

In one visit I had at the start of my practice, she kept shifting between figures that I have later identified as Isis, Astarte, Hecate, Asherah, Diana Lucifera, Artemis Diana, Durga, Kali and Inanna. During her shifting of appearances I asked her "-Who are you?" and she answered: "-Do you like me better this way, or in this way?"

At the same ritual, I also conjured up the "Lord" of Wiccan tradition. After a moment, I heard heavy physical footsteps closing in from another part of my apartment towards the circle. They seemed to stop right in front of me. Then I felt a physical hand grab my shoulder and the visions began.

I saw a falcon circling above me, descending towards me while it morphed into a man with an eagles head.

The whole room dropped in temperature while I watched him morph between figures that I, after the ritual, identified, as Cernunnos, Osiris, Ra, Apollo, Enki and many others. During all of this, he asked me:"-Who do you prefer that I am?", and smiled.

When I reached my hand across the borders of the circle of power, it felt like i was sticking it into cold water. The air was thick and heavy of spiritual and magical energy. I felt something physical grab my hand in a loving, caring touch.

They kept speaking to me about how they, and their representatives, had tried to guide and interact with different individuals in the history of mankind. How they had changed and adapted their appearances in order to make these individuals more accepting and willing to listen to their words.

They never wanted cultures to make war against each other, or to kill each other in their names.

The purpose was to help and to guide mankind into a higher state of conscious. Into a more viable existence on earth were humans could evolve into something better than themselves. To give mankind a chance of becoming members of an intergalactic, interdimensional society of unity, honor, respect, wisdom, strength, love and truth. The seven pillars in the foundation of the unity of light bearers.

It doesn't matter who you love, what you believe, how you dress, what you think, what you say or what you eat, as long as you carefully nurture these seven pillars that holds the union. But, if you break any of the pillars, you are not allowed to join the collective.

However, a loving father, or mother, would never close the door for his or her children. And there is no greater pleasure for a loving parent than when the blackest sheep of the family returns home to his family. So, never judge anyone, or anything around you. Let them judge themselves through their actions.

Never have any daults about whom, and what you are. The law is alive and written in the core of your soul. So, you will naturally do the right thing and follow these pillars if you listen to yourself. Know yourself, and you will know the way.

They wanted to gather each piece of the creational puzzle into the complete picture, so that everyone and everything would have the opportunity to try to comprehend the multiversian reality. Because full understanding of it, is impossible.

Each and every piece of the puzzle is very important, no matter how insignificant it might seem when it lies alone at the table in front of you. All pieces are needed to see the whole picture. The forbidden fruit must be eaten to achieve full understanding.

Isn't it to raise oneself above the gods and goddesses, when you stone another human being for breaking one of the "laws" that you, yourself, interrelates as the divine truth?

If all men and women were created in the image of God, How could you then kill a part of him, claiming that your own part is the only right one?

As I remember it, one of the guidelines was:"-Thou shalt not kill."

How can you forget about this while you carefully remember and shape other guidelines after your own personal interest?

Both men, and woman are needed to keep evolution on earth, so how can you blame one of them as "the original sin", and value one above the other. Is it because you don't like your own gods plan, and want to adapt it after your own personal interests? Or is it because you, yourself, don't trust woman?

Think of it for a moment, in ancient days, woman used to be considered necessary for divine interaction. Just think of the wondrous oracles of the Pythia in Delphi and a few other places. The high priestess was the representation of the goddess on earth, as seen on depictions from Paleolithic cultures all over Europe.

If you have this in mind, it is very easy to see why the established church wanted to keep the women out of any significant office of their faith.

A mainstream psychotherapist would certainly brush these visions away as a psychological manifestation of anima and animus. Something from the darkest corners of my own primeval mind and will. The problem is, that these entities often comes in full physical manifestations with a will and personality of their own. I often disregarded them as such myself, until I started to see them in the presence of other witnesses, or after watching simple video recordings done during their visits.

The gnostic secret of re integration is a mending of male and female energies to evoke the creative energy. And how can that be done in any other way than with a sexual, or spiritual union between the genders? Here I should mention that your soul is genderless or hermaphroditic in nature.

According to my own experience, sexual magic is the most powerful magic to be found in this realm. When you understand it and its implications, you will be able to create wonders not only in your bed, but all around you.

The influence of religious thoughts always makes me think that "-Aren't we all our own antichrists, if you want to find him, just take a look into the mirror. You are your own greatest and only enemy in your own spiritual evolution."

There's no darkness or light. The sun takes life as well as it gives life. So, it is a matter of perspective in how you look upon what is good or evil. Everything has its own purpose and function in this creation, or multiverse. None is better than the other.

A good example of this, is the ancient fertility Goddess Astarte, turned into a male malicious deity called "Astaroth" when the "new religion" started to gain influence in the upper political classes of east Rome.

They even went so far that they practically destroyed one of the ancient wonders of the world. The Diana temple at Ephesos, in modern day Turkey. There they also took the ancient images of the Goddess holding her child, and turned it into Virgin Mary holding Jesus. The veiled mother goddess became Virgin Mary. The lunar goddess Isis became the mother of Christ, Horus.

Another good example of archetypical influence is the "Noah" figure witch is told by a higher being to prepare himself and his loved ones for a great flood that will cleanse the world around him.

The same concept of antediluvian, or pre- deluvian cultures can be found in ancient stories like the Sumerian songs, the tablets of Sumeria and later Babylon tablets, and various interpretations made by many cultures from different times and places around the world. Here you will find the oldest versions we got of the stories about the trees in the Garden of Eden, and about the deluge itself.

It is easy to understand the foundation of this mythology if you think of the effect upon this world when the kilometer thick blanket of ice suddenly melted and raised the level of the seas around a major part of the world somewhere between thirteen and ten thousand years ago. The seasonal flooding's became worse for each year that passed.

Many of the existing societies then were deeply affected by its impact upon their environment and kept the memories about this disaster through mythology and religion. The effects of this disaster were imprinted upon our collective subconscious forever.

Some "worlds" were drenched by the following floods and much of their flora and fauna changed seemingly from one day to another.

Many of the "Atlantean" legends originates from these events.

A few of today's religions claims that their God is the only god. They have a monotheistic belief system that they usually claim is the oldest and most accurate one.

However, if you trace them through history and archaeology, it seems that more ancient monotheistic systems have been practiced in feks Egypt during the reign of pharaoh Akhenaton during the 14th century b.c.

In his new capitol, we can still read, upon one of the cliffs, something that seems to have inspired the ancient Hebrew bible, the "hymn to Aton". Parts of it is almost identical to psalm 104 in the old testament.

Considering that the story about Moses tells that he grew up in the court of an Egyptian pharaoh, it is very easy to see the connection. He must have been part of the cult of Aton that where widespread across Egypt, during, and shortly after the death of pharaoh Akhenaton. Solis sacerdotibus, the sun priests.

The following pharaohs fought hard against this cult as it worked against the temple institution that controlled society in those days. It was all a matter of politics and the agenda of power hungry people. Just as we see in current times within the church and other religious institutions. If you want to know the future, study history. It repeats itself constantly.

The "Moses" figure made himself an enemy of the political power that ruled the nation he was working in. So, the first of the "Levites" had to flee and find another place to dwell in. In order to do so, he used his knowledge about ritual high magic to convince others about his truth. For an advanced ritual magician it is not hard to send out plagues to a whole nation. And considering his upbringing in the Egyptian court, he must have had extensive training in ritual magic's and spiritual wisdom from the highest of sources at that time. In those days, it was a common practice to school your nobility in those areas from a very early age. After all, the king represented God on earth.

If I think about my own development within ritual high magic's, I have manifested great floods, storms, earthquakes, deaths, volcanic eruptions, starvations and tornados. And it taught me that it's not so important what you do, but how you do it, and with what purpose you manifest these disasters to others with. The greater disaster you would manifest for someone, the harder the slingshot effects would affect you if the purpose and intent wasn't pure enough from the start.

This means that if you embark upon this road, you will be punished so severely spiritually and physically that the magic itself would become pointless for you and your surroundings.

With great power comes great responsibility, as Spiderman's uncle told Spiderman before he died.

The "Athon" deity that the ancients worshipped, was a solar deity, the king of the sun. And he is felt when you study the "Lord" of modern, as well as ancient witchcraft, in all of his traits.

With this in perspective, it's very sad to study the history of the roman and Spanish inquisition and their crimes against humanity. Or when I see Islamists cut the head off from Christians and spiritual people on video clips that they send out to the media in these times. Why can't they understand that we all come from the same source, the same source that we will one day return to, and become one with.

I have, myself, seen this deity manifest as a large "moving star" coming down to a meter above ground, guiding me through the pathways of an old cemetery while speaking to me. Or as what some might describe as a "pillar of fire" while teaching me about philosophy and spiritual matters. I've seen him on many occasions and in one of those in the presence of another witness, manifest in the middle of a bush, or a tree, with a large golden, fire like appearance, that don't burn the tree or bush itself.

This only makes me more sad as I study how different religions fight each other, and thereby themselves because of the words of others that have had the joy and pleasure of interacting with higher dimensional forces in more ancient days.

If you start to experience miracles like these when you perform magic's, remember to carefully weigh your every word that you say to others about it. They might turn the words against you and mistreat them in horrific ways to emphasize themselves and their own existence.

I'm still wondering why an almighty and perfect God would order you to cut off a bit of your own penis to show him your devotion. Didn't he create you in his own image, as a perfect being?

If you study ancient texts about spiritual wisdom like feks the Arbatel, they said that the words between you and the deities were supposed to stay between you and the deities. They usually promised all kinds of spiritual punishments if you would reveal your conversations to another soul. I certainly understand why this warning was added to many of the ancient texts of magic and spiritual wisdom.

When it comes to the reality of interdimensional beings and the spiritual realms, I already know the truth, my truth. I will not waste my precious time in trying to convince anyone else about it. You must find your own truth by walking the way yourself. I cannot walk it for you, I can only point out some of the ways you can take towards the mountaintop were enlightment and wisdom is to be found.

But it is a very rough climb, and the higher you come, the harder it will be.

I can show you some of the tools in my toolbox, but you must build your own temple.

Just like in alchemy, you must arm yourself with wisdom before you start your journey. Read anything you can get hold on when it comes to ancient and spiritual texts as well as in the latest findings within astronomy, quantum mechanics, biology, psychology and history. It is all connected. Enlighten yourself with the wise words of old philosophers like Plato, David Hume, Pythagoras, Soren Kirkegaard, Marcus Aurelius (in my opinion the wisest ruler of the roman empire), Confucius and Aristotle.

Nowadays, we live in a very favorable time for magicians and spiritual explorers as it is perfectly legal with philosophical experimentation in the western world. It is easy to find most of the ancient, well known texts and grammars on the internet, for free. You can read anyone of them without risking persecution and burning at the stake.

The "new age" wave is not a bad thing spiritually, it is quite the opposite. Magicians today have more opportunities for self-development than in any other age before.

In the old days, you were lucky if you could get hold of one of the more doubtful systems developed from the keys of Salomon, or a pamphlet with magical seals most likely invented by its author just to make money and reputation. If you sought the path of a magician, you had to travel and meet other magicians to find knowledge about the subject just as Abramelin did a long time ago. Today it's just a click away on Google.

As I see it, all of the dimensions lies in layers on top of each other. Much like a Photoshop image is constructed. The bottom layer can usually not see or interact with the layer above. But the layer above can see and interact with the layer below. And this goes like a long chain through all of the layers of this creation.

Through the ritual modus operandi, every part is important to activate, through archetypical symbolism, different parts of the brain that you normally don't use. You activate your higher conscious and gain access to the collective unconscious.

Each instrument of the art activate a different portion of your brain through your senses. So think of this when you prepare for magic workings. Try to involve as many senses as you can. And also remember that the temple along with all the implements is also there to make the ritual area a more fitting area for the entities that you conjure up. The closer the temple resembles to the realm that the entity are called up from, the less energy the entity will have to waste upon establishing the connection and manifest for you.

The invocations themselves, are most effective if you, after much study and experience within ritual conjuration, write them yourself. This way they are easier to memorize. They will fit better into your own personal system of belief, and they will affect your own archetypical sense of spirituality better.

It doesn't matter if you are a Christian, Jew, Catholic, Muslim, Pagan, Hindu, Buddhist or atheist. In the eyes of higher dimensional beings you are just a child trying to find out who you are.

The more confident and sure you act during the ritual, of course without overestimating your own part, the more and grander the results of your experiments will be. If you say the wrong thing at the wrong time during the ritual, don't worry, just smile and take it from the start again.

When you reach a state of enlightment, one of the first things that you will notice is a strange feeling of "oneness". And with this I don't mean the oneness that the new age school use in so vast terms today.

It is a state of conscious were you reach the so called computer station, and have access to all of the information sent to it.

You feel and experience through everything that exists in this multiverse. Your connection to everything will become clear in an instant. And it is impossible to describe this state for another being that haven't been there for himself.

You become one with the source energy of this creation. Here I should mention that ignorance is bliss, in the sense that after reaching this state of mind, it is nearly impossible to adapt into a normal living. You will never look upon society and your fellow mankind in the same way again.

The path of the magician, is actually a path towards enlightment. A path that leads the neophyte towards master. A path for the individual soul to find its way back to the way it was created in the first place.

The old scriptures states that God created man in his own image. This is a very accurate claim, as we all have "the divine spark" within. A master magician have found this spark and uses it to celebrate himself and to improve his own as well as the life's of others. By performing the magic, he celebrates and honor his origin and purpose. He assimilates into his creator form without concern for his own ego. And with it, comes the realms of true magic and power. It will become more and more rare for him to perform magic to help his own development, than what it is for him to help others. The "creator energy" does that to you. And this form of energy is what lies waiting for you at the top of the mountain. So don't be disappointed when you find true magic power, as it will help others instead of yourself.

When you understand why, it will turn and start to work for you as well.

The greatest test you will be confronted with, is when you are about to "cross the abyss". Then you will have to be willing to sacrifice yourself for the betterment of others. If you chose to do so, you will pass without problems. If you don't, you will be forced to start all of your incarnations charges all over again. You might even have to incarnate as a rock again. So think carefully about the intention of your magic. One day you might be asked about it, and at the crossroad of the abyss, you will most surely be.

When I started to experiment with high ceremonial magic, I started with some heavy duty old system workings like "the heptameron", "the grand grimmoar", "the legemeton", "the grimmoare of Honorius" and "the arbatel". And it didn't take long before I was summoned before a higher being similar to what mankind today define as God. It wanted to know why I was doing what I did. My answer was simple but true. -Read my heart, you know it better than me. And through that you will see that I have no bad intention but the opposite. I just want to connect all the pieces of the puzzle, so that we all can at least try to comprehend the beauty of the creation in its true form.

I was then asked if I was willing to be banished forever for this.

I answered; -Just curse me however you want, as long as you support me in this, as it will help all beings, creatures, entities and energies from all the dimensions and worlds.

Three days later the god form sent a messenger to tell me that he liked the answer very much, and that he had decided to support me. After all was done, I would be welcome whenever I wanted.

This was a classical example of how the higher dimensions tends to send different tests to magicians that captures their interest.

All things, material as well as non-material, concuss as well as unconscious, is connected to something much like what Carl Gustaf Jung describes as the collective unconscious.

This connection is there because everything in this multiverse have a common form of intelligent energy that permeates it all. String theory does not work without the existence of a multiversian reality. Science will soon catch up with alchemy and old school magic's when it concerns other realities and dimensions. As it looks right now, the higher dimensions is hidden through the micro cosmos. Through the micro cosmos you can reach into the macro cosmos. Meaning that when you find a way into the micro dimensions that hides the gate into the macro cosmos, mankind will be able to travel dimensionally through most of the creation. Time and space would become relative and a no definable theorem that must be left as comprehended, not understood.

You can compare this connection to a vast computer station with lots of laptops connected. All of the data from the laptops constantly sends towards the common memory bank in the computer station. Through this connection, each and every laptop can, through the main source, connect to any one of the other laptops and communicate with the one behind the keyboard.

If you think of it in this way, you can easily see how it works with telepathy, mindreading, telekinesis, clairvoyance, spell works and other so called phenomena.

Science will soon merge with what people today define as magic when quantum mechanical experiments starts to reveal the reality of other dimensions and energies.

Personally, I enjoy to see how different theories in physics try to explain what magicians, cabbalists and alchemists have known for millennia's. It is not a universe, it is a vast and infinite creation of multiverses, all connected to each other. And they are all transmuting themselves into something else in their evolution.

Time and space is not relative, and the speed of light is not a border. So the possibilities of exploration are endless. The only limit is your mind and the rules you set upon yourself in exploring areas beyond that limitation.

What scientists today define as intelligent life, is just a bread crumb in a whole chain of bakery's. If you want a loaf of bread, you must rise from the floor, and start exploring the tables. And who knows? It might turn out that you are actually in a gingerbread house.

Introduction into archetypical and symbolical thinking

The flaming sword

Never give a sword to a man who cannot dance. :Confucius.

The sword, dagger or athame of the magician, is one of the most important symbolical instruments used during magical operations. So to start with, you should understand at least parts of the most simple of symbolism of what the sword represents for the ambitious magician.

When metal became more widespread and swords started to be constructed with it, the sword took over much of the same symbolism as the feather represented in ancient cultures like for example during the Egyptian old kingdom dynasties.

At that time, the feather, shut, represented divine authority, justice, mental abilities, judgment and the element of air. Shu, was the Egyptian god of air, and the father of earth.

In the afterlife, the deceased's soul, or heart, was weighed against the feather of Maat, to see how just the soul had been during its incarnation on earth.

The element of air represents speed, strength, mental qualities, spirituality, eternity and the male god form. During many of the enochian ceremonial conjurations you start the ritual by the eastern cardinal, or quadrangle when conjuring the circle of power. The archangel Raphael is the first to be evoked during most of the Goethic, catholic and old system magical grimmoars. The eastern cardinal represents death and resurrection from the underworld in the west. When the archangel Raphael manifests, he usually does so in bright yellow, or golden light. His energies are felt like a cold mountain breeze of golden healing light.

During most of the sabbatical workings within the craft, you also start the conjuration of the circle of power in the eastern cardinal were the ancient horned one resides.

To begin with you must start by analyzing the shape and form of the symbol.

The sword is made from fire, in a furnace. The blacksmith sticks the glowing sword into the ice cold water as a last stage in its construction, fire and ice. When he do that he also unites masculine and female energy into one force, creating a child, the sword itself. The glowing sword represents the fiery male solar deity, and the water filled pot, the cool lunar female deity.

The cooling sword represents Horus, the child of God and Goddess united as one. The Geburah, or the sword of God, justice and judgment. The magicians right hand during rituals and magical performances. It is the extended will and power of the magi.

In ancient cultures the sword was considered to have its own soul and personality. In some of those cultures it was common to give the sword a name and then treat it as a higher being. The keeper did not chose his own sword, it was the sword who chosed its keeper.

The sword was most often passed down from father to son, so the spirit of your ancestors was considered to inhabit the blade of the sword. With each and every blow you delivered, you did it with all the power and might of all of the ancestors of your bloodline.

This phenomena is very obvious in Asian cultures, but it can also be traced in European societies through myths and legends like feks in the Arthurian stories about Excalibur and the magical sword in the stone.

Here I should mention that during the process of manufacturing a sword in the ancient world, you poured the melted iron into a stone mold, and when the iron cooled down a bit, it stiffened and you could draw the new sword from the stone.

Only a true and just ruler can draw the sword from the grip of the mountain.

The sword was initially bestowed upon mankind from the lady of the lake, the goddess, unto a magician that would guide its fate among the lives of mankind.

The symbolism of the sword coming from the reflective, mirror like surface of the lake also shows that you must know yourself before finding the higher wisdom, represented by the sword. A reflective look upon your life and soul must be done if you seek the fire of Prometheus.

When you know the basics of western esoteric alchemical tradition it is easy to see the archetypical symbolism in this story.

The sword laid a firm foundation to many of the superpowers in the early history of mankind. Only the rich and powerful could afford to gather iron and make it into swords. At first, the swords were made out of copper, and then someone found out that if you mend some tin into it, it would make the sword stronger. Bent and broken swords was a common thing during times of battle. The one with the strongest and sharpest sword would rule the battlefield. The technological race to conquer the enemy was as intense in ancient days as it is in the modern world. There's no coincidence that mankind seem to evolve most during times of war, at least in technology.

If you want to become a light bearer, you must have a true and just heart in order to lit the spiritual flame that enlightens your soul. It demands a unity between darkness and light, a spiritual maturity that leaves all judgment into the hands of god and goddess. All things comes from the same source and contains parts of the creative higher energy.

From chaos comes order, from darkness light and after day comes night. All forces and energies that inhabits this creation, or multiverse are necessary for its completion. How could darkness exist without the light, and the opposite way around.

There are no black or white magic only magia naturalis, natural magic. It is the magicians perception about himself and his own magic that forms his opinion about the nature of his actions. Darkness and light is a matter of perspective and what is dark for some, might be light for others. All things are on an eternal path of transmutation towards evolution of itself, and during some of these metamorphoses the traveller will go through phases that seem very destructive and chaotic for others. The magician must explore all forms of magic, he must know how to use both hands when lifting heavy weights.

He must gather all the pieces of the creational puzzle in order to try to comprehend the bigger picture and thereby catch a glimpse of the nature of its creator, the great architect or initiator. Exotic matter is intelligent and permeates all material in this universe and others. This connects all manifestations in all universes into a multiverse. It creates new dimensions to realities that transmutes other planes after their own perception about them.

Conscious thoughts manifest itself into new realities in other realms. In other words, if you believe in a fiery pit called hell, then you will also manifest it in the astral plane to begin with. What manifests in one plane affects all the others, as above so below.

A good example of this is the creation of lodge egregoirs and how their power and strength grows with the number of members and their abilities. The personality of each member forms the egregoire and its nature.

Just as among the twelve gods and goddesses of the Olymp, each member should have different qualities in their personalities and abilities to form a powerful and wise manifestation of its purpose. Only then could the members find re integration if they all work in peace with each other towards it. Many small streams can form a great river if they unite as one. And at its end a great lake could form by its sheer size and strength. But also have in mind that the mental status as well as ethics and philosophy of each individual member, will affect the same qualities in the group egregoire.

Some of the astral entities also make a fine example in this context. Are they manifestations of faith and mythology that comes to life just as an egregoire do? If so, think of the consequences of horror movie villains when many souls keep transmitting images of them into the collective subconciuss.

Another good example is the so called role playing games that were popular when I grew up. In these games that you play with a group of people, you make up characters and whole worlds for the game itself.

The point is that all the characters and worlds you create during role playing games comes to life somewhere in this wondrous and infinite multiverse that we sail through on a constant journey of transmutations.

Thoughts are creations that manifest into their own reality through the will and power of the operator. These manifistations comes into action through words and invocations that directs the creation towards a purpose. It is the basic foundation of magical practice.

The same principal can be viewed upon in a very clear sense if you think of how many of the old temple practices were performed. Most often, the participants re enacted a celestial event in order to manifest the beings concerned in these practices. During these re enactments the participants also evoke different parts of their own brain, much in the same sense as the magi does during goetic rituals. They evoke, within themselves a stronger bond and feeling of the entities conjured, this technic strengthens the magic in many ways. You re create and connect to a particular energy from a chosen time and space into the ritual scene. As I have already mentioned, it is very important to adapt the ritual scene as much as possible to make it as easy as possible for the summoned beings to connect and manifest in the same spiritual and physical realm as the magician.

These phenomena can also be studied and understood through paranormal investigations were they use so called trigger objects from the time and space of the entity that the investigators are trying to establish physical contact with.

The way of the goetic magician should include stages from all of the qualities found within the goetia if the so called true magic is the goal. The path is an alchemical transformation of the magicians soul and personality. The magician will become the philosophers stone when he reaches his destination and finds his own true will that illuminates his soul.

In alchemy the process starts when the alchemist produce a form of prima materia, a base material witch he transmutes towards the last stage were it becomes the philosophers stone. It is as much a physical as it is a spiritual journey to fulfill the opus magnum of an alchemical path.

However, the great work can be achieved in many ways, magical transformation of ones soul through ritual high magic is just one of them.

This is also one of the reasons to why I recommend you to evoke all of the 72 angels of the goetia at the same time, to find balance in the personal power awakened during the ritual. Each and every entity will affect the participants psychologically and spiritually with its own energy and functionality when they connect and manifest into this realm. The more you work with them, the more they will affect you. Personally, I summoned all of the 72 angels each time I performed a goetic ritual, even if I just needed to speak with just one of them for a particular purpose.

I also take the time and effort to communicate and greet each and everyone of them during these performances. If you do this, it will also strengthen your bond to all of them. It's a way of showing respect and thought to all of the entities that signed my goetic book of contracts a long time ago. As I treat them all as important friends and family, they do the same towards me.

Of course you could achieve astounding results if you provoke and threaten these entities during the conjuration, the question is if you will recieve a negative or positive effect during the operation and after you close the temple.

A sense of good moral and ethics without any form of ego that will pollute your soul and work against your opus magnum is essential. Otherwise you will not have the strenght to draw the magical sword from the hard grip of the mountain king. Arm yourself with wisdom before you start the quest. Listen to Merlin, your higher self, when guidance is required. God created you in his image and that means that you are also God in your own reality.

The Lord of the mountain knows your heart better than you will ever do, so make sure to study the mirror closely before you start the spiritual quest of Percival. Know yourself, because you are your own greatest enemy on this journey. Otherwise, you will end up like Homers Odeusseus that could not find his own harbor again after the wars at troy. In his case, I take his pride as a wise warning that spiritual psychosis is very real and present for anyone that speaks to the gods and goddesses.

Have mercy upon yourself, how else would you be able to have it for others. In secret, we often judge ourselfs and our own actions harder than anyone else.

When you start your spiritual journey, you must do it as a newborn infant. Forget about your past and make a new foundation for your own personality through spiritual wisdom and conclusions done from your experiments. These conclusions can never be found through the study of other masters workings alone. Be your own star, and follow it without a dault.

Use what is good for you and don't be used by others to do what is good for them.

You are the greatest master of your own spiritual path, and if anyone says otherwise run like hell. No one knows your own true path as well as you do, remember that.

On this journey, there are no rules except your own moral and ethics. A true philosopher don't need any rules, he follows them anyway.

Your destination will be formed by your path, so just remember that when you walk upon it.

Use the muddy slides and strong winds to strengthen yourself, not to bring yourself down. You will need the strength when you reach the top of the mountain, because the winds are pretty strong up here.

The most common initial shape of the sword is the one that forms a regular cross when the sword points downwards.

It is formed by the heath of the fire, and thereafter it is used as a cold blade. Fire and ice united in the same symbol.

The blade reflects light very clearly, and if you hold a sword up high, it will reflect light from its blade. You will become a bearer of light.

It is also of great importance that you understand the importance of metal in the ancient days. A piece of metal shaped after your own purposes in those days, meant that you had divine power and could control it for your own purposes.

It meant power and authority over not only the forces of nature and the spirit, but also over your surroundings. During the time of the first swords made out of bronze, the Neolithic population looked upon this phenomena as a mythical thing. Many tried to make copies of swords out of simple flint rock. The sword represented divine and secret wisdom, as well as divine power and authority.

In the dance of life, the tarot, the sword means power over mental and psychic abilities. In a sense, this is what it truly means. And it is easy to see for an adept within the area.

When Adam and Eve was thrown out of the garden of Eden, they were chased out of it by many cherubims armed with a sword of fire. At the eastern end of the garden were the tree of life stood, it was carefully guarded by a flaming sword. No human were ever supposed to enter there, at that time or place.

The sword meant divine intervention, authority and so on. In a more flavored version we can study the symbolism by adding the attributes of the sword and of the element of fire. Then we can continue to add the symbolism of the tree of life and of Cherubims. And not to forget that the tree stood in the eastern end of the garden.

In the outher level of masonic practice, the meaning of the sword is most obvious if you look at the guardian of the temple.

In the start it was a guardian supposed to protect the master of the lodge, and later it turned into a charge to keep the profane and curious from the rites. The guardian was supposed to keep all the profane away from the rites. And therefore he was the only one allowed to wear a sword during the rituals. His function was to stand before the entrance to the temple, with sword drawn, defending it from any form of hostility and profanity.

Never sheath your sword without honour used to be the torch of earlier lightbearers within the craft. In order for you to understand at least part of this truth, you must understand the significance of the meaning of the sword in those days.

It used to be a common part of your gentlemen suit so to speak. As a gentleman you had to wear a sword. And if you represented the royal agenda, you would most probably have an unsheathed sword in your coat of arms and during rituals. To carry a sword meant that you had honour and wisdom to wield or sheath it when the time was right.

The sword is a solar phallic symbol representing the male deity, its sheath the lunar female deity.

The magic mirror

She had a magic mirror. Every morning she stood before it, looked at herself, and said: Mirror, mirror, on the wall. Who in this land is the fairest of them all.

To this the mirror answered: You, my queen, are the fairest of them all. Brothers Grimm, Snow white.

Just as the story about Percival or Odysseus the fairy tale about Snow white and the seven dwarfs is an excellent story for psychoanalysis and archetyphical symbolism. It is easy to see that the evil witch suffers from a narcissistic personality disorder that drives her towards her own doom.

The same type of phenomena tends to linger around the magician when he starts to experience true magic for the first time. The experience is so overwhelming that the magi will naturally put himself above all others. He will commit hubris against his own divinity. It is a natural process that each magi must go through in his own evolution of self exploration. There is a reason to why Jacob, in his vision, saw a ladder, and not an elevator to heaven, so to speak.

Some practicioners will be struck by a state of the Jerusalem syndrome and never get out of it.

It is always good to aknowledge your divinity, identify with a god, or goddess form if you have to, but never assume that you are the true essence of that god, or goddess. It is just ridiculous and disrespecting to do so. And it is precisely what cursed many ancient heroes into an eternity of suffering in Tartarous. The mirror reflects many truths, not only your own. It can show what is behind you, to your sides, above and below you, with its image.

Another approach towards the Delphic words of wisdom, know thyself, is that you must know your own limits. Know that you are human and not God, as some of the mystery schools taught their pupils in ancient Greece, or as the wise Enoch wrote about the so called fall of the lightbearing angel that according to mythology wanted to become higher that the most high. See upon each part of the creation as a piece of the same puzzle, and study the symbolic meaning of the ancient texts.

The first traces of the use of mirrors can be seen in Egyptian hieroglyphs depicting female subjects admiring their reflection in handheld mirrors, probably made out of copper. In ancient Mesopotamia polished copper mirrors can be dated as far back as about 4000 b.c.

Before copper and bronze mirrors, simple ponds or lakes where used for scrying and evocative rituals. Then people started to use cauldrons filled with different liquids usually mixed according to the cabbalah or something similar.

The elusive and reflective surface of lakes and ponds became a transformative place, a point of entry between the realms and people started to make sacrifices into them.

With this in mind, it is easy to see the connection to when the goddess usually manifests out of the reflection of the moon upon a small pond in a forest clearing in the astral realm.

The mirror used to be a symbol closely connected to the goddess Venus, Aphrodite and Isis. Its element is water and its ruling planetary body the moon and mercury.

It is also important to remember that the light we see from the moon, is actually a reflection of the suns rays. We can see the moon because of a symbiotic relation between the lunar surface and the suns light. This force comes through our eyes that translates and interpretates it into an image in our brain. Darkness and light, united as one force, and with the eye, a trinity. So, always have in mind that what you see and experience, might not be the same as others, even though you describe it in a similar way. All things is a matter of perspective.

When looking upon how we use mirrors today, we can, through simple symbolism see what they mean to us.

When we wake up in the morning, after a nice cleansing shower, we study ourselves in the mirror to see how others look upon us. It will always tell the naked truth to its audience.

When we drive to work, we study whats behind and at our sides through the mirrors. We can even see the hidden dangers behind corners in front of us.

When coming to work, the collegues that surronds us mirrors different parts of our own personalities, just as your own family and loved ones do. We manifest the reality that surrounds us, weather we want it or not.

Conjured manifistations in a magical mirror will reveal itself with a reflection of the karcists own personality and level. This does not mean it is manifistations of the magis own psyche. The entities called upon will take on the appearance that represents the will of the magician. You get what you ask for.

This also means that you should read the descriptions about the entities with a grain of salt, and place more weight upon the symbolic descriptions of their offices. And the stronger faith you have in their reality, the more physical manifistations you will have both during, and after the rituals. Study the pantheos and entities that you will conjure up, learn as much as you can about them before you try to summond them. This shows respect not only to them, but also towards you as a magician. It tells the other beings that you are serious in your quest. And trust me, they have seen so many bad efforts in trying to conjure them through the centuries.

It is also important that you know that it is very rare with a full physical manifestation of the entities in the magic mirror. I see the mirror more as a portal, and a point to focus during the conjuration. It is normally used in goetic magic, placed upon the center of the triangle of manifestation, to help the operator, or pilot, to induce a trance like state were it is easier to see the spiritual entities through psychic abilities. However, it is possible through hard work and much training, to learn how to find the right focus in your eyes so that you can see the entities and higher dimensional energy through them instead of psychic imagery.

Your own emotional status will mirror itself in the magic you perform. If you are very dark and angry you will find it easy to conjure the entities that goes hand in hand with the purpose you are seeking to manifest. Just remember that your personality will change into that of the entity you conjure if you are not aware and vigilant against it. The risk rises for each time you keep conjuring the same being, so find balance by conjuring all of them at the same time, or shift entity for each time you conjure.

By now, it should be easy for you to understand that the best and most powerful magical mirror is the one that the magician constructs himself. The more energy the magi puts into its creation, the more powerful it will become.

The aestetichs behind its design will be a trademark for the magician in the other realms during ritual conjurations. Its shape and markings will reflect the power and wisdom of the magician behind its making. It will assist its constructor in opening up and activating the right portion of his brain in order to communicate with his higher self and thereby to interact with higher realms. However, a powerful magician will be able to transform the physical mirror into a portal and gateway for other dimensions that even a neophyte can take advantage of. Never underestimate the reality and value of true magic.

The mirror can be constructed in a fast and modern way if you get hold of a good photo frame with a glass plate. Any well sorted supermarket usually have them for an accessible price.

Then you just need a spray can with a dull black color, some thick black paper and a good gold color pen.

After this, you take out the glassplate, spray paint it with many layers of the dull black paint on one side, and then paint the whole frame with it.

Then you cut out fitting pieces of the black paper to follow the inner line of the frame, surrounding the point of manifestation in the glassplate. Take the gold pen and write one fitting divine name, according to your preferred pantheon, on each side of the frame, so that the names encircle the area of manifestation.

Construct the mirror during a full moon, or if possible during a blue moon, to add more power to its purpose. You can even leave it were the fullmoon will shine upon it, for a night, to charge it with its energies. If you do so, you should cover the mirror with a black or red silk cloth immediately after, and keep it covered unless you are working with it.

If you are a practicioner of the craft and know how to draw down the energies of the moon, planetary bodies and the stars into vessels, you should do so into the mirror. And you can place the mirror on the northern cardinal during Sabbaths and rituals. It is the cardinal ruled by the gnomes and the element of earth. The cardinal where you call upon the goddess, or the archangel Auriel during evocative work.

The nature of physical manifistations

Angels, and ministers of grace, defend us.
Be though a spirit of health, or a goblin damned.
Bring with thee airs from heaven, or blasts from hell.
By thy intents wicked or charitable.
Thy comst in such a questionable shape,
That I will speak to thee.

Shakespeare, Hamlet 1. 4

Physical results produced through the efforts of magical rites can appear in many and various ways. They rarely come as you expect, and even more rarely when you expect them to come.

However, even though magic is a science that is, at its best unstable, some form of unity can be found in the product of ritual evocations.

To begin with, we have the bodily symptoms that will affect you when you are in the precense of extra dimensional beings. Their higher frequency will be felt in many ways that are not always that obvious for the neophyte. Every time higher beings are active around you, they will manifest many bodily symptoms that usually have the same type of appearance, a common driving force. The effects can, in some cases, last for months after the operation. With time and experience you will learn to recoqnize them all without any daults.

These forms of manifistations are also indicators of your magical success in many ways. If you are successful and the entities respect and honour you, you will never experience threatful or harmful manifistations towards yourself or your loved ones. When they do manifest, it is to strengthen and comfort the magician with their physical precense.

Quid pro quo, something for something, the magician gets confirmation that interdimensional beings are affected by his work. A little bit like the idea of hanging a carrot in front of a donkey to make it walk somewhere. It is never the magician that decides when, where or how a manifestation will take place. It is always the beings manifested that are in full control of the situation.

If the magician is righteous and have a good set of moral and ethics the entities will respect and listen to him. So, if the magician follows the simple steps of the seven pillars of the union, he will have nothing to fear from interdimensional beings or their manifestation of power in this reality.

Treat them all as close family, and they will do the same to you. For that is what you really are. We all come from the initiative thought that became manifested into the reality of this creation through the will and intention of the same creative force or energy that permeates all physical and nonphysical material.

This effect can be easily studied by the magician in the creation of beings and worlds in the astral realms, and how the same comes into manifestation in the spiritual world. This is done through the magicians use of his "divine spark", the creative energy. "…when God created man, he did it in his own image…" is a very good paradigm to describe what is happening. To use it is not a sin, it is a celebration. To use it wisely is a sign of respect and honour towards it. And to enjoy it, is to embrace and cradle it as a newborn infant. So carefully nurture and grow your own spirituality as an innocent infant discovering itself and the surroundings it inhabits.

Carefully think of Pandoras box, Ulysses, and of the Djinns in "Arabian nights". The latter is a warning about working with the 72 genies of King Salomon. It shows the traps and dangers when making a wish, or sending the entities at work for personal interest. The opening of "Pandoras box" might seem innocent, but might also provide havoc and gore around the curious opener. All that was left was hope.

Ulysses thought he was equal to the Gods, and got punished to never finding his home and family. If you go into a psychosis with the "Jerusalem syndrome" you will most surely lose your home and security. Listen to the wise words of ancient knowledge preserved in mythology and nighttime stories for ages.

Some of these beings are a "force majeure", a true force of nature, a higher power. And they must be treated with respect for that.

I have a few case studies among previous students were the karcist is very proud of how "his" entities perform various forms of physical attacks upon his loved ones when he is angry at them.

The truth is that in those cases the entities are not doing this out of respect for the karcist. It is more a sign of disrespect towards the magi and his loved ones. A proper relation with the entities conjured is shown in their treatment of the magi and his loved ones. No matter how harsh arguments that arise between the magi and his family and loved ones, the spiritual entities should never react with violent actions to neither of them.

If the magi starts to experience scratches or any form of harmful events, he must take a break from the ritual performances of magic, and focus on what went wrong.

He must take the time to go through his own psychological development as well as the ritual modus operandi itself. The fault lies in one, or perhaps both of them.

Case study 01: before and after being introduced to this form of Goetic magic.

Male, 20- 25 yrs of age

- Had minor symptoms of psychological disorder. Paranoia, psychotic and irrational thoughts. Showed clear signs of a deep depression with many dark thoughts about himself, and others.
- Spoke with a very low voice during conversations.
- Suicidal dreams and fantasies about harming himself.
- Minor abuse of psykofarmaka and lighter drugs like Cannabis Sativa, and a chemical copy of the latter drug.
- In the upper scale of normal to excessive intake of alcoholic beverages.
- His fear and low self esteem manifests in an obsession of weapons and marshal arts. Constantly seeking approval from others through his conversations about knowledge in weaponry and fighting technics.
- Has a fear of emotional attachments to family and others that often manifests in threats and violent actions to anyone that he feels attached to.
- Obsessed with the darkest parts of magic, like for example necromancy, Satanism, ritual sacrifices of either human or animal nature, just to mention a few.
- Sadomasochistic imagery of a sexual nature.
- Submissive self-imagery in denial of his masculine self as an indicator of sexual abuse in an early age. This is also shown in his urge to mark his own body with cuts and burn marks.
- Very introvert personality.

Case study 02

35- 40 years of age

- Signs of a compulsive personality disorder manifesting in his obsession of how his surroundings persieve him. Comes from a poor and hard working family in a poor European country.
- After many years of hard work he established himself as a successful director in his own company.
- Severe narcissistic personality dissorder. He can stand in front of the mirror for hours before going outside and he spends a fortune on pheromone potions in order to attract and get the attention of others.
- In the upper scale of normal to excessive intake of alcoholic beverages. No use of other psycho stimulus. But over uses medical herbs and remedies.

Bodily manifestations.

When a higher vibrational entity comes close, you will feel it long before it happens.

You will feel watched, like something is carefully studying you from a distance. It's a feeling that reminds of the one that a prey must feel in the presence of a predator, even if it is a peaceful meeting with a friendly entity.

This is partly because most entities conjured are usually so much more vast and ancient than what the karcist is.

It is very common to feel threatened by the sheer size, wisdom and power of the beings conjured. When you start to understand these beings and your place in the creation, you will not feel threatened by them any longer. But you will always feel the vastness behind the eyes that are observing you with an unexplained curiosity from the incense smoke that surrounds you during the rite.

The next feeling that usually follows when you conjure is the sense of coldness when the entities starts to draw energy from this dimension in order to manifest results that binds the realms together in a unified effort to produce a manifestation of the magicians desire.

Temperature changes is a very common phenomena that most magicians experience during the peak of a ritual.

At this stage of the magic operation, the magi may also start to experience unexplained gusts of winds, tapping sounds, knockings, pokings, phantom smells and grabbings.

The more intense the phenomena becomes, the more he will feel the energy used for the manifistations. This usually starts with a burning sensation of higher energy flowing through the spine towards the neck, and then it follows the sides of the head towards the third eye.

The phantom smells most often comes from ozon created when the portal opens between the realms. It is most often mistaken for the smell of sulphur and brimstone, especially if the karcist is a devoted Christian or Catholic in his or her belif system.

If the energy and intensity of the rite rises now, the magician will most probably start to feel nausea, dizziness, headaches and a high pitched sound piercing through his ears.

It is at this stage that the magician can drive the conjuration all the way towards a physical manifestation of the entity. He is just about to hit the first note of the crescendo.

The magicians feelings and conviction about the ritual will be closely entwined with the results of his performance. If you don't belive in the reality of the beings that you call upon, why would they manifest in reality for you. You get what you ask for, especially if you ask for it subcouncioussly remember that.

The first sign of an entity that is about to manifest during the ritual is a loud knocking or tapping sound, usually coming from a place between the eastern and the western cardinal.

At this point, the magi will start to feel a rising energy of bliss. Here it is very important that the magician is aware of the stage that the ritual have reached, and that he, with it, raises the intensity of his voice and movements. If he do so, a full physical manifestation is achievable through the entities gathering of particles in the incense smoke that should lie like a thick mist in the whole temple.

The next that happens is that he will start to feel an altered state of happiness and joy. No matter what darkness that will manifest, he will still see upon it as the most beautiful thing in the creation. He will be in a state of divine love and bliss for all things and beings.

You will feel like a God, but remember that you are certainly not that.

What happens here, is that the magi starts to access his Godhead, his higher self, or as Crowley and many others call it, he finds his personal holy guardian angel. Personally I have three guardian angels, Baltazar, Melchior and Antonious, but what I mean here is more the personal higher self awareness of the operator. The realization of oneness with all things, beings, entities and energies in the creation. A calm breeze of knowing the creational energy and its purpose in context to your own existensial whereabouts. Spirit, matter and wisdom as one, a trinity of evolutional transmutation towards the beginning and the end of excistance.

The next stages of manifestation are usually the spiritual and astral visions sent to the magi. He will see an image of the conjured entity with his third eye.

At times, the entity might chose to send visions of sacred geometry or symbolism that speaks to the magicians own archetyphical senses. It is, feks, very common that the enochian deities and kings manifest images of pyramids, squares and spheres when the magician summond them. The symbolism reflects the level that the magician is currently on. If he is an experienced and powerful magician the archetyphical messages will be conveyed in perfectly clear images unto his higher self.

The more you speak a language, the more you will understand the broader meaning of every word spoken. But the first time you conjure up an entity that manifest himself in the image of a hook, a Junipher tree or a pyramid, you will have serious daults about the images that you receive. When this happens, just look for the symbolism in the manifistation. The images are meant for your higher self so no one else can help you to decipher them.

If the beings chose to come in symbolical images, the karcist can ask the entities to show themselves in a more understandable form, if that is what he desires.

This is a critical stage of the magicians personal evolution, as it is here that he confronts himself and his own abilities. Does he accept these visions as sent from higher beings, himself, or just as another psychological phenomena?

The day that the magi accepts, with heart and soul that these phenomena are sent by external forces, he will start to manifest physical results during this new stage.

During this step, he will probably be confronted with lightphenomena or something likely during his daily life. His reaction will determine the further outcome of his magic.

If the reaction is positive, he will start to have physical light manifistations on a daily basis, along with tapping sounds and various of other phenomena occurring all around him. Invisible grabbings and pokings all over the body becomes more normal than not. And various poltergeist phenomena becomes more and more common all around you.

So, it is very important that the magi is stable psychologically before starting upon this journey of self discovery. Otherwise he will surely turn into a deep state of spiritual psychosis very fast, and from that, it is almost impossible to recover ever again.

Common physical phenomena around the magi after great operations with the goetic system.

Tapping sounds, knockings, light streaks, light glimpses or orbs, shadow figures, phantom smells, strong day or night visions, poltergeist phenomena, sounds of claws upon hard floors, disembodied voices either astrally or physically, sense of smell and taste gets emphazised. Headaches, shaking hands and tics, prickling electrical sensations in the hands, and at times all over the body. Along with all of this comes a variety of many other phenomena.

Depressions and extreme mood changes with dark thoughts and actions. Paranoia, selfdestructive behavior, stomach problems and negative delusions about your own surroundings will constantly be in your mind.

When the magi is in the precense of an extra dimensional energy or entity, his soul will recognize the higher energy and identify with it. The core energy of the soul will naturally try to vibrate closer to the frequency of the otherworldly energy. Similar attracts similar.

If the magician is a very young soul, the gap will be to great between the energies, and the magi will experience very strong bodily symptoms and sicknesses. In the worst cases he can be drawn into a coma like condition, but it is more common with dizziness and nausia, followed by nightmares and sleeping problems during a month after the ritual performance.

It is also common with uncontrollable astral traveling, day or night visions and fluctuations in energy as the souls vibration becomes unstable until it has adapted into a new frequency.

The souls new vibration will blur the borders to dimensions close to this. So many otherworldly beings and energies other than the ones called upon will be drawn towards the magi. He will be living his life on a stage, so to speak, performing for an invisible audience.

This can drive the magi into developing different states of paranoia, not only from the metaphysical, but also from the physical world.

The evolution of the magician is as much psychological as it is spiritual in nature.

What to do when confronted by dark effects

The first thing that the magician needs to do when he starts to experience negative effects from his magic, is to find self control.

The entities can, if they don't respect you, affect your mood and behavior towards the ones that you love and hold dear. They can make you forget to pay bills, to reach important meetings or agreements that will be of positive effect to the karcist.

After the first conjurations, most of you will find that you are behaving very aggressive towards people and situations that you thought that you would never act negative against.

So it is very important that you are aware of this effect, as you can then take control of your own actions by not following the impulses that will otherwise take control of your life and spirit.

In paranormal investigations, the investigators are most often using recorders to catch electronic voice phenomena. At times they manage to document very clear voices of, in most cases, human voices that can speak and answer to questions in an intelligent way.

When otherworldly beings affect the behavior and mood of a human, they can speak directly to them, repeating over and over again words that the human only hears through his subconciouss. This way the human starts to think it is his own thoughts and reacts to them without being aware of it.

Find balance after the so called dark magic by performing white magic. If you conjure demons one day, make sure to conjure angels the following day. This helped me very much on my own path, as the negative effects never got the opportunity to work on me for a longer time after their manifistation into this realm. Be aware of your own actions towards others in the days after working with this form of magic.

I always try to teach that you are your own greatest enemy on this journey, and that is very true, especially if you let something else to take your decisions for you. It is a sign of weakness in the other realms. Learn how to rule over yourself instead of others, that's where you will find true power.

Truth is higher than any religion, so always contemplate what you are confronted with with an objective and curious heart. Be aware of when other beings are trying to make you see upon everything around you as hostile and negative. When you are aware, you are also the one in control. The next you need to do, is to update your spiritual and magical protection, both physically and spiritually.

If you are a devoted catholic, make a visit to a Sunday mass. And if your system of belif is another, just focus on that system for a moment. Never neglect your own true faith and path through this incarnation. The more truth given, the more truth is received. If the operator was raised in feks a catholic system, it is already imprinted upon his subconciouss mind, and can create a conflicting personality as a magician towards the system that he is working with.

Practice energy meditation daily, as this will strengthen your personal level of defence and adapt your spiritual bodies into its new vibration faster.

Do good things for those in most need of it. This will help to clean up the carmic effects a little bit. Stop looking for a solution elsewere with other witches and magicians, find it yourself as it is your own homework. If you don't solve it yourself, what would you do the next time it happens.

A magician always takes the hard path to learn and to build strength from it. You don't let others do the homework for you.

Bless and consecrate your house and grounds with sandalwood or Sai baba insence. Walk around its borders with incense lit, saying, I bless and consecrate this sacred space in the name and honour of the Lord and the Lady, while envisioning your footprints glowing with white energy.

Do the same while sprinkeling water and salt from your last full moon Sabbath in front of you.

If the lucid dreaming becomes too much for you, draw a pentacle, and write the names of the four cardinal angels, on virgin, unused paper, and place it under your bed. This will protect you and calm down the interference in your dreams for a short moment. To charge the seal, just keep it in the center of your circle of power during ritual workings.

For spiritual entities it is easier to connect with this realm if the reciepent is asleep. It takes less energy to reach into the subcounciouss of the receiver when he is in a state of rem sleep. This also counts for negative and harmful entities and energies. So, the magician is always most defence less during his sleep. He is most likely to be under attack then.

These entities prefer to do their workings somewhere between 0300 in the morning, and until sunrise.

However, the best remedy is to try to try to understand and interpret the hidden message behind your dreams. Remember that in the dance of life, death means transformation, so never judge a horse by its teath. It is very easy to miss interpretate the messages from beyond, just think of all the kings that came to the oracle at Delphi before their major battles.

Light manifistations

The light phenomenas or manifistations are most common outside in the nature during starclear nights. Then the entity can draw energy from an outside source for its manifestation. When its starclear it can draw energy from the star that vibrates in the same frequency as its own energy and use it to produce a variety of light phenomena. The sources can be many.

During the blue moon in December 2010, at new years eve, I had many entities that visited as large light orbs were they drew energy from the fireworks in the area. This also affected the nature of their manifistations. They seemed to use the same color of light as the majority of the fireworks surrounding us. However, to be noted, is that the manifistations were usually of an orion or plejadean origin. The light orbs were mainly made out of solar and fiery energy.

At other times I have seen them do the same thing with a simple street light. Most of the times that they draw energy from street lights or electrical devices, their electromagnetic energy will severely affect the apliances ability to work for a very long time after. Street lights will flicker and computers will shut down or freeze. During my darkest periods of experiments, even the lights in the stairway had a perfect and constant horror movie flickering in front of my door.

If an entity is of a solar, or a plejadean origin it will manifest in a golden or orange light orb, streak, glimpse or apariation. And if it is of a lunar, Sirius or mercury origin, it will come in a bright blue, silvery light manifestation.

A divine being will always come in a bright white light that radiates a feeling of love and bliss. Earthen elementals always manifests in bright green, or brown lights, just as dark beings most often comes as red or blue lights.

The creative force, or the precense of the great architect, the source, usually comes as light glimpses. If you are outside during starclear nights it will show as lightning like manifistations without sound. The whole area around you will seem to lit up in fast flashes of white light.

He also likes to manifest bright blue light orbs or light streaks across the sky.

One time, as I walked my nightly rounds on my security job at an old cemetery, after a night of enochian magic, I had a pleasant experience with the creator.

I walked as usual, a couple of times per hour, along the fence of a diplomatic building, but this time something extraordinary occurred. When I closed in to a set of bushes, everything became brigthly illuminated. There was a bright light shining straight upon me from an unknown source a few meters above my head. The ground beneath me was suddenly lit up in a perfect circle of white light. I looked at the source of light, the unexplainable opening of light from a higher dimension. My eyes got blinded from the it, as I heard the voice of the creator.

He is not the vengeful and evil force that you typhically read about in ancient texts. He actually have humour and a loving curoiusity towards all beings of the creation that is uncompaired and not comprehendible by a single soul.

As I have seen him many times, and got to know him very well, not only from this life, but many others. I would like to describe him as a mixture of Zeus, Yawe, Odin and Ea. He usually comes as an old white haired and bearded man with piercing blue eyes. When I meet him in his own dimension, he usually sits upon a throne sourunded by cherubim like beings and light orbs. The surroundings are usually composed of pure white light and mist.

He is the king of the mountain, the magician and creator. Our lord, in the sense that his energy is part of our own soul and everything that surrounds us.

Anthropomorphic or animalistic manifistations of extra dimensional entities

A picture says more than a thousand words.

The sorcerer, cave painting from France, estimated to be from somewhere around 13 000 years ago.

The Gundestrup cauldron at the national museum in Copenhagen, Denmark.
Estimated to be from somewhere between 200 BC and 300 AD

Amun Ra, King of the gods and creator of the universe, from a tomb in Luxor, Egypt.

Moses, Michelangelo, tomb of Pope Julius II

When I started to conjure in a wider scale, I noticed how I suddenly had wild cats following me around when I was outside, birds flew close to, and in front of me.

Dragon flies and butterflies started to come close, as if they wanted to greet me and thank me for what I did in my magics. To begin with I simply disregarded these phenomena as a form of brain spooks and coincidents. But after a few years, it became more evident that after each time that I conjured in a larger scale and interacted with higher beings, anthropomorphic and animalistic manifistations was a reality. I could not deny it anymore. In the start they came as visions and dreams, and later as fully physical phenomena.

Today I know the truth very well. And it is one of the hardest things to describe unto the neophyte.

Training makes master and no training makes no master

In order to successfully communicate, and interact with interdimensional beings you must train your spiritual and astral senses daily. The more you train, the more powerful magician you will become. There are way to many armchair magicians out there that thinks it is enough to read a couple of books, and then successfully perform a ritual from one of them. It does not work that way.

To be a magician is a very hard job that demands much training and many failed experiments before you start to notice satisfying results. To be a magi is also to have reached a higher level of conciouss after much development of your soul through many past incarnations.

It is rather pointless to conjure up a spiritual being if you cant communicate with them or even hold the visions that they will send to you. Its very respectless towards the entities that you call for, so, I recommend that you start training all of your spiritual and astral senses daily. It doesnt have to be a complicated thing to do.

To begin with its important for you to understand that your spiritual senses and abilities is relaying much on the frequency and vibration of your souls core energy. So, one of the keys to raise yourself towards a greater potential, is to raise your frequency, to work with what you have in energy and to raise it after your best ability. Training makes master.

Some are born with very high energy and strong spiritual abilities, but without using, or training them, they will soon weaken. It can be compared to bodybuilding in a sense, its just spiritual bodybuilding.

First, its very important with some spiritual and philosophical understanding, as this is also a thing that will add to raise your core energy.

So, a good thing is to start looking at religious mythos and philosophy from all over the world, and from all times. Dont limmit yourself here, try to find the thread between the cultures and times, for it is there to be found.

A good start can be to select a deity, from one of the most ancient cultures, and then try to find deities with the same symbolism and persona, through each culture and time. Then study how the deities develope after the needs and expectations of the cultures were they appear. Theres not one creator, there are many creators, and one initiator. The creators often shift appearance and names with different cultures and times. In ancient times, people used to call the creators, watchers. They knew that some of these creators, at times incarnated in human form to help and to guide mankind through history. A good example of this, are the greek and norse mythos.

Study ancient texts of spiritual wisdom, and majical grimmoars. You can feks start with the Arbatel and the wisdom of the ancients. These texts are easily found on the internet, just type in grimmoar, or sacred texts in google. Look upon them as pieces of a great puzzle, were you have to gather them in order to see the picture grow forth in front of you.

Along with this, you should look at history in a global perspective, try to find the thread through it, and to see how it has developed in stages.

Take a peak at psychology, and different theories durings its development. Here I can recomend C.G. Jung, and his masterpiece about archetypes and symbolism.

Never stick to one theory, keep on walking through the academic jungle as a newborn on a spiritual adventure.

When you start your practical training, so to speak, try to implement bits and pieces from what you have learnt in your studies.

You could feks start to use sound therapy, to easily and fast get your brain into a delta, or theta level, so that you know how it feels. This way you can also reach it fast and easy by yourself later. You can easily find nice pieces of soundtherapy to reach these states of conciouss on youtube. Listen to it as much as possible at start, to train your physical brain in the feeling of it.

Personally I used to listen to it with headphones constantly, feks when i took long walks outside, or just when i meditated, witch i did for a couple of hours every day.

Have in mind, that the more you train, the faster and higher you can climb without falling down again.

I will here mention a few easy technics to train and develope your spiritual senses, do the training as often as possible. Develop the technics after your own abilities and needs.

1. Energy flow and visualization

Put some nice and relaxing music in the background, to help your mind relax and to give you something to focus on so that your mind doesnt run away in thoughts during your training.

Shut off all electrical lights, and your phone. Make sure that none disturbs you for at least forty minutes.

Sit, or lie down comfortably.

Close your eyes.

Relax your body, bit by bit until you feel it tingles. Start to focus on your feet, and legs, work your way up through the whole body.

When you are completely relaxed, start to visualize a large glowing ball of light above your head. See how it sparkles with white and lightblue energy. Envision a sparkling, electromagnetic sound from it, you can even feel the smell of ozon coming from it. Try to feel how its energy radiates upon your physical and spiritual bodies.

Do this for some time, until you feel it very strongly.

Step 2.

Envision how a beam of light slowly comes from this ball of light, towards your head, and fills up an area between your eyes with its light. Then it flows straight through your whole body, towards your feet, and on its way, it lits up first, your throat, then your chest, pelvis, knees, and finally your feet. At the same time, it also flows through your arms towards your hands and lits up your palms with the same intense color and energy.

Try to envision how this energy flows through your body, and keeps on circulating your whole system, from the large ball above your head.

Step 3.

Hold your palms towards each other, with a distance of appr. a decimeter. envision how the energy flows through the whole system and towards an area between your hands, forming a little ball of glowing energy between your hands.

Try to feel and explore the prickling, warm sensation of the energy that grows in power between your hands.

Step 4.

Place a vessel in one of your hands, feks a stone that you like, and do the same, visualize how the energy forms a glowing ball of light in the middle of the vessel.

Use this vessel in your further training.

Step 5.

Now place the vessel between your hands, charging it, while you envision the energy as fire. Try to feel the heat, hear it sparkles, and how the smell of fire fills your nostrils.

Take a deep breath, and when you slowly blow out again, slowly vibrate...-Beeeeh iiiiii teeeeyyyy oooohhh eeeeehm - (Bitom)

Call out mentally:Djinns and Salamanders, spirits of fire.

Step 6.

Do the same as above, but now envision water, a stormy sea, and how water flows through your body, and hands, into the vessel.

Slowly vibrate :-Heeeee seeeey ooooh eeehhhm aaaay- (Hcoma)

Call out mentally: Undines of the water, spirits of water

Step 7.

Same as above, just envision earth, and dirt.

Slowly vibrate :-eeeehhhhnnnn eeeey eeeehhnnn taaaaaay- (Nanta)

Call out mentally: Gnomes of the earth, spirits of the earth.

Step 8.

Same as above, just envision air, and winds.

Slowly vibrate :-eeeeyyyy eeeexxx aaaaaahhh eeerrrr peeeeey- (Exarp)

Call out mentally :Sylphs of the air, spirits of the air.

Do this often to get a feeling of the different elemental energies, and to learn how to channel them.

2. Crystal vision and 3rd eye vision

Crystal vision is the ability to see through all the ethers with your physical eyes. And with 3rd eye vision, you see through the realms with your "inner eye". Its an ability were you see spiritual things and entities through inner visions and dreams instead of using your bodily eyes.

It is a great advantage to have both of these qualities, and to train them constantly in preparation before any old system magic ritual.

To achieve crystal vision is no harder than to focus your eyes after awakening from an intense dream. After the first few times you have tried it, its a matter of seconds to adjust your eyes focus to penetrate the ethers. But it takes training and practice as often as possible to get there. And when you do, you will see the goetic entities with your physical eyes, their energy imprint upon this realm, even if they dont manifest in physical form here.

When I grew up, i used to skygaze at a very early age. In fact, among my earliest of memories are from when I do that. When we went fishing on small mountain lakes during winter time, I used to lie down on the ice and scry into the sky above me. After some time, I started to see shapes and beings forming from the small dots of energy particles that permeated the air all around me.

3. Preparation.

The temple and ritual area does not have to be a complicated thing to set up. It is quite enough to just put candles in the right colours for each cardinal in their right place around you, in a circle.

Everything you do, other than that, will raise the power and virtue of your ritual. So, just do it as good as you can. Just remember that all magics comes from within. The tools and rituals are there to help you remember and to focus into your higher concioussness.

Nowadays most magicians perform their ritual workings in a regular living room, in their apartments. And it is usually done, in such a way, so that they can hide any trace of the workings from one day to the next.

It is very important to remember what conditions the magicians of ancient days faced. They had to be very inventive in the construction and preparation of the rites and of the instruments to be used in them. If someone would discover any trace of majical workings around them, they would be tortured and meet certain death in a horrible way. So they used everyday material as their instruments. They could feks use a regular kitchen knife as an athame, or sword of power. Then they just inscribed the knife with colors that would be easily removed with water.

Even the smell of incense can be a problem for some of the practicioners, and if such is the case, just use a consecrated stick incense.The best is, of course, if you could fill your ritual space with a thick and heavy layer of smoke. The entities called upon, can then gather the particles in the fumes in order to manifest their shape in this dimension. The more the perfumes corresponds to the realm and entity called upon, the more favourable manifistations you will recieve.

You dont have to febreshly scream out your invocations (even though it helps). If necessary, just whisper them in a low voice.

Remember that in ancient days when these entities were called upon, it was usually, a carefully hidden secret, preformed by people in very sensitive places ranging from monks in different monestaries into covens of witches and magicians meeting up in a desolate place of the closest forested area. Discovery would most probably mean months of mind boggeling torture followed by a slow death in a public display.

Also remember that it is better to master one technic perfectly, than thousands of technics that you barely know how to perform. The ritual modus operandi, is just a technic, a tool, to be used in order to focus your mind and attention upon manifesting your will from one realm into another, and to clearly show the dimensional beings and forces that you call upon what you wish to have assistance with, and how you want that assistance to be given.

The envisioning technics are used not only as a mean to communicate telepathically with interdimensional forces and beings, but also as a mean to communicate and activate your higher state of mind. The divine self, your soul.

In a sense it can be compaired with riding a bike. Your mind envisions what your body should do, and it does it. You work with your spiritual and astral bodies in the same way. When sending out mental images and commands, you also manifest those images and commands in the collective subcounciouss, and throughout there unto any force, being or energy called upon.

Everything in this multiverse, or creation, has a spark of prima materia, the creative force, or energy wich is connected to the source of creation, the initiator.

With this in mind, it is easy to understand that the ritual begins at the moment that you decide to conjure a particular being. The time that you spend drawing the enitites seals, is a time were you start connecting to the enities. The more work and energy you put into making the seals and to prepare the experiment, the more power you add to the creshendo of the ritual performance.

If you want the experiment to end up with as good results as possible, it is also important to always look upon these entities as real beings, with a personality of their own. Otherwise, you will just invoke the egregoire of the grammar, and, or, your own psychological archetype representing the entity you wish to summond. And trust me, it is a major difference when you reach this level in your majics. In my own oppinion, you havent really experienced real majics until you have reached this level. When you do, you will experience many wondrous moments were the entities actually manifests in real solid physical forms and lightmanifistations all around you. Most often they will do that within a couple of weeks after the ritual performances. And usually it will happen when you are outside, during nighttime, in an isolated place in the nature. But it might, as well happen in your own bedroom or kitchen when you least of all expect it to happen.

If you dont perform these experiments with honour and respect towards these beings, you will also start to experience the so called "sling shot" effects manifesting negative events all around you for months after the experiments. The entities will start to work against you instead of for you.

In a sense, you should percieve these majical rites as a form of spiritual politics were you are networking and showing your intentions each time you do a conjuration. So, dont proclaim yourself to be almighty and godlike when conjuring these entities, cause you are certainly not that. They know exactly who and what you are.

After a few years and hundreds of conjurations, you will start to develope personal bonds to many entities, not only from the goetic realms, but also from other realms and dimensions.

Each time you perform a majic rite, you are on a public display for interdimensional beings, so think of how you want them to know you already during the first experiments. Im not saying that they watch your ritual modus operandi for faults. They are observing you, and your intentions. It doesnt matter if you belive in them or not, they will still be there, watching.

This also gives a reminder that it is not enough to read others books about majics, you have to practice over and over again before the other realms starts to get to know you, and you them. When that is achieved, the work starts for real. Theres already too many "armchair magicians" out there today. And they all claim to know the only "right" way to a higher understanding and "majic power". As I see it, it is just a breath of these times. The new age philosophy of love and light were everything is ok as long as you keep your new age false holiness up front. This is a very bad way of entering the diplomatic scene of other dimensions. Theres no darkness nor light, it is just magic naturalis. Everything in this creation, or multiverse, comes from the same source. The sun gives life as well as it can take it, without being an evil force.

It is also important that you have in mind that the entities of the Legemeton, used to be worshipped as gods and goddesses in the past, until the church decided to name them demons and destroy the old temples of worship around the world. A good example of this is Astarte, the greek name of the semitic chief goddess, that turned into the male demon Astaroth when the church started to expand its political influence throughout the middle east. The name Astaroth has a more ancient hebrew influence, but the entity that the church turned this goddess into is far from the truth. Also have this in mind when youre reading the Legemeton. Its authors, was influenced by their times and values. Not to forget the dangerous times that they lived in during the writing of most of the"old system" grimmoars. Just as the prewords to the "Heptameron" (by Peter de Abano) in the fourth book of occult philosophy by C. Agrippa reminds us, when he makes the reader think that its just added to show a wider perspective of the belif of the ignorant and uneducated people. In reality, he was already preparing his defence towards the inquisition.

The grammars written about "old system majics" are usually written during times were you always had to make sure to not to say too much.

When you read the legemeton today, you can see the seals and names of power as the red thread that comes through many other grammars. The rest is usually the authors own personal majical system and values. The way, he or she have chosen to work with these seals and names.

You will need at least a simple understanding about how the different stars and constellations affects the outcome of the rites. So, I recomend that you study the kabbalah, at least to get a simple and basic understanding of its contents.

When I have physical lightmanifistations outside at nighttime, I often see how different entities manifest within the starlight of different stars, and in particular times when different constellations are visible. So, it is very important to use the doorways when they are open. You dont have to do this, but it will enforce your callings significantly.

When you prepare for a conjuration, you should always have in mind that you are also preparing the space, the temple, to be as similar to the entities worlds as possible. Feks, when you make sure to burn an incense that corresponds cabbalistically to the realm, or dimension that youre contacting.

You can empower this in many ways in order to make it easier for the entities to manifest into this dimension and world.

To begin with, you could feks use large glass candle holders in the same color as the candles you burn on each cardinal. This helps to make the space around the candles to vibrate closer to the realm of the elements that they represent. Similar attracts similar.

It is also a good idea to construct your own personal ritual incense. This way you not only do the best to give a good atmosphere to manifest in, but youre also leaving a form of business card in the other realms each time you use it. The entities surrounding you will know your intention each time you burn your personal perfume of the arts. It will be a familiar atmosphere during majical rituals.

The more perfectionist you become in your ritual technics, the more perfect results you will recieve. You could feks print out the enochian watchtower seals and make a frame of simple wooden sticks, forming a small cubic candle holder. There are many ways of empowering your rites, creativity is your only limittation.

I would suggest that you start your ritual performances alone, or at least with as few people as possible involved. We are all on a different level spiritually. Our souls energy vibrates in different frequencies depending on many things such as age and experience.

When you perform a successful operation you also raise your own vibration. Each encounter with a higher dimensional being will raise it further. Your soul will recognize the higher vibration and it will automatically try to vibrate closer to its frequency. This is most obvious during the weeks following a full physical manifistation. Then you will get hurled into a state that many magicians chose to call "divine bliss".

A higher vibration also raises your spiritual senses and abilities very fast. With this in mind, you might realize that it demands lots of hard work before you can become a powerful magician. There are no rites that will make you all powerful in an instant. First you must show, through your majical operations that you work hard for it. After that you can, if possible, get your promotion.

The magicians road is a desolate place, his journey is a very personal process of development and awakening. No one is better than the other, all souls are different and we all have different strenghts and roads towards the mountaintop. So, therefore, you must also remember that the most powerful majics, is when you are experienced enough that you start to form your own personal system of majics. Its just like Chinese kung fu. Build upon your strenghts, and disregard the rest. Its pointless to know how to do a roundhouse kick, if you do it bad and your right punch is more effective.

It is also important that you know that there are no borders between darkness and light, as most "new age" schools of majics usually claims that there are. The sun takes lifes just as well as it gives it, without being an evil force. It is all a matter of perspective. Never approach these rituals with the belief that it is about evil and malicious forces. If you do so, that is what you will encounter as an egregoire or a simple archetype of your own mind.

Holy water

To begin with, you need to consecrate water and salt. This does not have to be a complicated rite. You should use the invocations and prayers that you feel corresponds to you in the best way. Or, if it feels better for you, just pick up some holy water from the closest catholic church.

Personally i prefer to use the consecrations from "The grimoire of Lady Sheba", as it fits well with my own personal system of majics. Or, as more commonly nowadays, I just say "-I bless and consecrate thee, in the name and honour of the Lord and the Lady, and so mote it be, blessed be." Then I charge the water and salt with lightblue energy, while envisioning the words written with golden letters upon each. If I wish to empower this further, I just summond my closest entities from the element of water, for the water, and my closest earthen familiars to empower the salt. After this, I just drop a few pinches of salt into the water with the tip of the athame, and then I stir it a few times.

Dont complicate it, the more easy it is for you, the more natural it will feel for the entities involved. You can build upon your consecrations, blessings and invocations with your experience. The foundation is what holds the top of the pyramid in place. If you have any daults about this, just ask Pharaoe Sneferu about his early building projects.

Consecrating the incense.

Place the mortar with the herbs, or the stick icense in your left hand. Place the right hand above it and envision a ball of lightblue energy forming in the center of the incense, while stating the words of your consecration. "-I bless and consecrate thee, in the name and honour of the Lord and the Lady, and so mote it be, blessed be."

Lighting the perfume of the arts.

Envision how you pass on the lightblue fire of the element of air to the incense while you lit it and state the words: "-Now, my dear creature of incense, you burn in the name and honour of the Lord and the Lady, and you shall bring pleasing odours and energy to empower all majics and invocations done, when you burn, and so mote it be, blessed be."

3. Ritual modus operandi (ritual work book)

After you have prepared your temple and everything else that needs to be prepared before the ritual, you walk into another room to dress yourself in your ritual garnment.

While dressing, repeat the following prayer out loud.

> *"Ancor, Amacor, Amides, Theodonias, Anitor, by the merits of thy angel, O Lord, I will put on the garments of salvation, that this which I desire I may bring to effect: through thee the most holy Adonay, whose kingdom endureth for ever and ever. Amen"*

When you tie the rope around your waist, kiss each of the three knots on it while stating:

"In the name of the Lord, the Lady, and their son"

While you walk in a slow pace into the ritual room, and into the circle, chant the following:

"Artemis Diana, Ashera, Diana Lucifera, have mercy upon me. Kernunnos, Osiris, Apollo, have mercy upon me. Bless me now, and at the hour of my death, and so mote it be blessed be."

Take your bowl with holy water, in your left hand, face east, and then start walking clockwise three times around the circle, sprinkeling holy water around the circle, and upon yourself while saying:

"Purge me with hyssop, O Lord, and I shall be clean. Wash me, and I shall be whiter than snow."

Sprinkle the incense three times, with holy water (while facing east), saying:

"The God of Abraham, God of Isac, God of Jacob, bless here the creatures of these kinds, that they may fill up the power and virtue of their odours, so that neither the enemy, nor any false imagination may be able to enter into them, through thee the most holy adonay, the Lord and the Lady and their son."

Now, sprinkle the coal you will burn the incense upon (before lighting it), while saying:

"I exorcise thee, O thou creature of fire, by him by whom all things are made, that forthwith thou cast away every phantasme from thee, that it shall not be able to do any hurt in any thing. Bless, O Lord, this creature of fire, and sanctify it, so that it may be blessed to set forth the praise of thy holy names,

so that no hurt may come to the exorcisers or spectators, through the Lord, the Lady, and their son."

Light the coal while saying:

"Now my dear creature of fire, you burn in the name and honour of the Lord and the Lady, and so mote it be, blessed be."

Now put some incense to the burning coal while saying:

"My dear creature of incense, you burn in the name and honour of the Lord, and the Lady, and you shall bring pleasing odours and energy to all spirits, creatures, entities and energies that comes to my call, to protect, help, guide and support me, and so mote it be, blessed be."

Pick up the incense burner with your left hand, and start walking around the circle, three times, starting on the east cardinal, while saying:

"With these sacred odours, I bless and consecrate this sacred space and everything within, in the name and honour of the Lord and the Lady, and so mote it be, blessed be."

Sit down on your knees, facing east, and say out the following prayer:

"O vos omnes, adjuro atque contestor per sedem Adonay, per Hagios, et Theos, Iscyros, Athanatos, Paracletos, Alpha et Omega, et per hac tria

nomina secreta, Agla, On, Tetragrammaton, quod hodie de beatis adimplere quod cupio."

Lit the eastern cardinal candle and then stand, facing east, in worship position, palms up, while saying the following out loud:

"Now my dear candle, you burn in the name and honour of the Lord and the Lady, the archangel Raphael (vibrate his name), the element of air, sylphs of the air, spirits of the air, Exarp (vibrate this name: eeeeey eeeexxx aaaaahhhh rrrrr pey)."

Walk clockwise towards the southern cardinal, light the candle and then say out loud the following while facing west:

"Now my dear candle, you burn in the name and honour of the Lord and the Lady, the archangel Michael (vibrate his name), the element of fire, Djinns and Salamanders, spirits of fire, Bitom (beeeeyyyy iiiii teeeyyy oooohhhh eeeehhhmm)."

Continue towards the western cardinal, clockwise. Lit the candle and then say out loud, while standing in worship position, palms up:

"Now my dear candle, you burn in the name and honour of the Lord and the Lady, the archangel Gabriel (vibrate his name), the element of water, undines of the water, spirits of the water, Hcoma (heeeehhhh sssseeeeyyyy ooooohhh eeeehmm aaaaayyyy)."

Walk up to the northern cardinal and lit the candle, while facing north, and say out loud:

> ***"Now my dear candle, you burn in the name and honour of the Lord and the Lady, the archangel Auriel (vibrate his name), the element of earth, gnomes of the earth, spirits of the earth, Nanta (eeeeehhn eeeeyyy eeehhhnnn teeeyyhh aaaahn)."***

Walk up to the eastern cardinal, face east and start the following rite:

Stand in worship position while envisioning how your body reaches out to the limmits of space above earth. You see stars all around you, and after a moment a clear lightblue star is moving towards you, and stops right in front of you, hoovering in the air about half a meeter in front of you. Lift your right hand towards the star and draw it down towards your forehead while vibrating the name:

> ***"Atheeen"***

Draw its light through your body towards your feet, and through them into the earth core itself, while stating out loud:

> ***"Maaaalkuuuth"***

Now, place your right hand on the middle of your chest and draw the light towards your right shoulder while saying out loud:

> ***"Veeeehhhh geeeeburah"***

Place your right hand in the middle of your chest again, and then draw the light towards your left shoulder while vibrating the name:

"Veeeeehhh geeee duuuuhhhlaaa"

Now stand in worship position, palms facing up, while chanting out loud:

"Layyy ooohh laaahm aaahmen, layyyy ooohhh laaahm aaaahmen."

Stand still, in silence for a moment, envisioning how a large cross of lightblue light is radiating from within your physicall body.

Look towards the eastern cardinal while stating (vibrate the angels name):

"Before me stands the archangel Raphael"

Envision how the angel comes towards the cardinal point, surrounded by a purple and yellow light. Close your eyes and say out loud (vibrate the angels name):

"Behind me stands the archangel Gabriel"

Envision the angel walking up to the western cardinal, surrounded by orange and blue light. Turn your head towards south, close your eyes, and state out loud (vibrating the angels name):

"To my right stands the archangel Michael"

Turn your head towards north, close your eyes, and state out loud (vibrating the angels name):

"To my left stands the archangel Auriel"

"-Blessed angels, be my shield, be my sword, be my guide, and so mote it be, blessed be"

Face the eastern cardinal, and envision how a large pentacle in glowing lightblue energy is hoovering above each cardinal while stating out loud:

"Around me shines the pentagram"

Now, envision how a large six rayed star, a star of David, is radiating lightblue energy from within your chest, while stating out loud:

"And within me, shines the six rayed star"

Take a short break to refill some incense upon the incense burner and to study the seals, contemplating the entities you will call upon. Now is also a good moment to visit the toilett, smoke, drink or whatever you need to do before starting up the conjurations. However, the break shouldnt be longer than five to ten minutes, as you wait for the energy to build within the circle, and to give the entities, that youre about to call, the opportunity to show up and take a peak at the temple and the carcist. They already know that you will summond them, so they should already be present in the temple area.

Sit down in "lotus position" facing the eastern cardinal, place your book of contracts on the floor, or ground, in front of you. Take a few moments to contemplate the purpose of your rite, your charge to the entities. Envision how they show up to sign the contracts. The entities read your mind and while doing this you also instruct them about your intention before the call.

When you feel ready, start reciting the first goetic call, while, at the same time envisioning the entities showing up around the circle, ready to fullfill your charge.

Read slowly and vibrate all the names of power.

"The first goetic call (conjuration).

I invoke, summond and conjure thee... (study each seal, while stating the name of the entity), and fortified with the power of the supreme majesty, I strongly command thee by Baralamensis, Baldachiensis, Paomachie, Apoloresedes and the most potent princes Genio, Liachide, ministers of the Tartarean seat, chief princes of the seat of Apologia in the ninth region; I exorcise and command thee, all the 72 angels of the goetia, by him who spake and it was done, by the most holy and glorious names Adonay, El, Elohim, Elohe, Zebaoth, Elion, Escherce, Yod he vau he, Tetragrammaton, Shaday: do thou forthwith appear and show yourself unto me, here before this circle, in a fair and human shape, without any deformity or horror; do thou come forthwith, from whatever part of the world, and make rational answers to my questions; come presently, come visibly, come affably, manifest that which I desire, being conjured by the name of the eternal, living and true God, Heliorem; I conjure thee also by the particular and true name of thy God to whom thou owest thine obedience; by the name of the King who rules over thee, do thou come without tarrying; come, fullfill my desires; persist unto the end, according, to mine intentions.

I conjure thee by him to whom all creatures are obedient, by this ineffable name, Tetragrammaton, Jehovah, by which the elements are overthrown, the air is shaken, the sea turns back, the fire is generated, the earth moves and all hosts of things celestial, of things terrestrial, of things infernal, do tremble and are confounded together; speak unto me visibly and affably in a clear , intelligible voice, free from ambiguity. Come therefore in the name of Adonay, Zebaoth; come, why do you tarry? Adonay, Shaday, king of kings, commands thee."

At this moment, the circle should be surrounded by all of the 72 angels of King Salomon. You should start to recieve visions of how they move around you. Some may show you, in visions, how they sign a page in your book of contracts, while others will keep moving around you while studuying your reactions. You might also start to notice a few physical signs of their precense such as temperature changes, tapping sounds, phantom smells of sulphur and ozon, pokings and pulses of electromagnetic energy surging through your body.

Silently recite the lords prayer within your mind:

"Our lord who art in heaven, hallowed be thy name. Your kingdom comes and your will be done, on earth as it is in heaven. Give me this day, my daily bread, and forgive me for my tresspasses, as I forgive those that tresspass against me. And lead me not into temptation, but deliver me from evil. Yours is the kingdom, power and glory, forever and ever, amen."

Put some more incense upon the coal in the incense burner, and start to recite the second goetic conjuration out loud.

"Second goetic conjuration.

I invoke, conjure and command thee, all the 72 angels of goetia, the 72 angels of King Salomon, to appear and show thyself visibly before this circle, in a fair and comely shape, without deformity or guile, by the name of On, by the name of Y and V, which Adam heard and spake; by the name of Joth, which Jacob learned from the angel of the night of his wresting and was delivered from the hands of his brother Esau; by the name of God Agla, wich Lot heard and was saves with his family; by the name Anehexeton, which Aaron spake and was made wise; by the name Schemes, Amathia, which Joshua invoked and the sun stayed upon his course; by the name Emmanuel, which the three children, Shadrach, Meshach and Abednego, chanted in the midst of the fiery furnace, and they were delivered; by the name Alpha and Omega, which Daniel uttered, and destroyed Bel and the dragon; by the name Zebaoth, which Moses named, and all the waters and rivers in Egypt were turned into blood; by the name Elion, on which Moses called, and there fell a great hail, such as never was seen since the creation of the world; by the name Adonay, which Moses named, and there came up locusts over all the land of Egypt and devoured what the hail had left; by the name Hagios, by the seal of Adonay, by those others, which are Jetros, Athenoros, Paracletos; by the three holy and secret names, Agla, On, Tetragrammaton; by the dreadful day of judgement; by the changing sea of glass which is before the face of the divine majesty, mighty and powerful; by the four beasts before the throne, having eyes before and behind; by the highly wisdom of God; by the seat of Basdathea, by this name Primeumaton, which Moses named, and the earth opened and swallowed Corah, Dathan and Abiram; do thou make faithful answers unto all my demands, and perform all my desires, so far as thine office shall permit.

Come therefore peaceably and affably; come visibly and without delay; manifest that which I desire; speak with a clear and intelligible voice, that I may understand thee."

After this conjuration, you should sit down and think through what you wish the entities to do for you, and then you envision how they are all signing their names in your book of contracts. Then adress the entities out loud:

"Welcome noble angels. I humbly and respectfully ask of thee to come forth and sign these contracts for me. That you will come to help and assist me, whenever I may open this book of contracts with thee. In return, I will light candles and incense for thee, each time I ask for your precense. And so mote it be, In the name and honour of thee, blessed Lord, and Lady."

Now thank the entities for coming to you, and for performing their charge. Say that you are greatful that they will do this for you, without causing any harm or negativity towards you, or anything that you love and hold dear. Tell them to go back to where they came from, and to be ready to come whenever you call, or open the book of contracts.

Then repeat the "Cabbalistic cross ceremony" to close the rite and cleanse the temple again.

Walk up to the eastern cardinal, face east and start the following rite (the cabbalistic cross):

Stand in worship position while envisioning how your body reaches out to the limmits of space above earth. You see stars all around you, and after a moment a clear lightblue star is moving towards you, and stops right in front of you, hoovering in the air about half a meeter in front of you. Lift your right hand towards the star and draw it down towards your forehead while vibrating the name:

"Atheeen"

Draw its light through your body towards your feet, and through them into the earth core itself, while stating out loud:

"Maaaalkuuuth"

Now, place your right hand on the middle of your chest and draw the light towards your right shoulder while saying out loud:

"Veeeehhhh geeeeburah"

Place your right hand in the middle of your chest again, and then draw the light towards your left shoulder while vibrating the name:

"Veeeeehhh geeee duuuuhhhlaaa"

Now stand in worship position, palms facing up, while chanting out loud:

"Layyy ooohh laaahm aaahmen, layyyy ooohhh laaahm aaaahmen."

Stand still, in silence for a moment, envisioning how a large cross of lightblue light is radiating from within your physicall body.

Put out the candles (counterclockwise through the circle), starting with the eastern cardinal.

Wrap up your book of contracts in a black silk cloth and place it upon your altar for the rest of the night.

Astral conjuration of Goetic entities through an incense portal of salt.

Now, this technic is for the more advanced magician that already got extensive experience with astral travelling and conjurations. With this experience, it is a technic that can become much more powerful and personal in nature.

The magician travels astrally through a spiritual portal and brings the entities from their realm into this, through his spiritual, astral and physical bodies. Due to this form of modus operandi, the entities will affect the magicians soul, or energy in a more intense and powerful way. It is therefore very important that the magi have complete self control and no mental problems, otherwise it can be devastating to the magician in many ways.

If you are prepared for this mentally and spiritually, you will have a greater opportunity for more physical experiences, and the entities will be able to affect and control events in this realm more easily with less energy spent while doing that.

Arm yourself with wisdom before embarking on this road.

As the magician becomes more experienced, and starts to build a reputation in the astral realms, he should develop and form this ritual after his own personality and abilities.

The first thing you need to do is to create a sacred space for you in the astral realm. See this space as diplomatic grounds were all that comes in peace are welcome.

Personally I have set up a large Christmas tree forest with high mountain tops, deep rivers, and a large glowing pentacle in a forest clearing. This is were I do most of my astral conjurations, and the entities knows the place and purpose of it very well.

Physically, you will need this:

- 1 half a coup of consecrated salt
- Some holy water
- 24 riverstones with a letter from the futhark written on each one of them
- 1 black ink pencil
- 1 piece of blood red paper
- Stick incense, preferably naq champa, or red wheat (red sandalwood)
- 1 shot of vodka, whiskey, cognac, or red wine as an offering to the entities conjured
- 1 shot or glass of vodka, whiskey, cognac, or red wine for yourself
- 1 black or red candle
- 1 cup of holy water (to drop the burning invocation in when you burn your fingers)
- 1 checkerboard colored pillow

First you need to physically prepare the ritual and yourself.

Start by taking a long shower and while you do this try to envision how the water cleanse you from dark energy while stating:

With this water I bless and consecrate myself, in the name and honour of the Lord and the Lady. With this sacred water I bless and purify myself in the name and honour of the Lord and the Lady.

When you dress yourself you say out loud:

I dress myself in the garnments of salvation, so that wich I want will come to effect, in the name and honour of the Lord and the Lady.

When this is done, you start by making a circle of salt, 30 to 40 centimeters in diameter, on the floor, facing east. Then you place the riverstones upon the salt circle so that it is surrounded by the sacred futhark. Here

I would recommend that you learn the essence of the futhark so that you can place the signs connected to the Lord on the left side of the circle, and the signs connected to the Lady on its right side. And the seal of the demon either on the right side of the portal, or around your neck.

Place the candle and the cup of holy water on the right side of the circle, and the shot of vodka, congac, or red wine on the left side of the circle.

Place the checkerboard colored pillow in front of the circle, so that you can sit on it during the conjuration.

The holy drink:

Face the eastern cardinal. Lift the glass up high in front of you, envisioning the drink glowing in a bright white light.

Move the glass towards your forehead and then towards your feet. Then back towards your chest, to your right shoulder, then the left shoulder and raise it high in front of you while stating: To the Gods and Goddesses! Drink!

Next you write the invocation for the spirit that you will conjure up.

Invocation to be written on the blood red paper, with the black pencil:

In the name and honour of the Lord and the Lady, I summond and conjure thee …. (name of spirit)

I summond you in the name and honour of love and light, so that you may come in all of your power and might, to fulfill my desires without causing any harm or negativity towards me or my loved ones.

Come (name of spirit), come forth and reveal yourself unto me, come and answer my request for thee, and so mote it be, in the name and honour of thee, blessed Lord and Lady.

The words that you need to repeat after burning the invocation in the candle flame are: Come (name of spirit), come forth and reveal yourself unto me, come and answer my request for thee, and so mote it be, in the name and honour of thee, blessed Lord and Lady.

After the holy drink, you need to open the portal.

First you bring the stick incense towards the altar candles. Light it first on the Lords candle and then the Ladys candle, while stating out loud: Now my dear creature of incense, you burn in the name and honour of the Lord and the Lady.

Then you move towards the salt circle and trace a large glowing golden pentacle above the ring of salt, while stating out loud: Now my dear creature of incense, with these sacred odours I bless and consecrate, charge, empower and open this portal to the other realms, in the name and honour of the Lord and the Lady, Arida and Kernunnos, Diana Lucifera and Lucifer.

Sit down ontop of the checkerboard colored pillow in front of the ring of salt.

Focus for a moment while envisioning the entitiy, and what you wish it to help you with.

Read out loud the invocation on the blood red paper, while holding it up high with your right hand three times. Then burn the invocation in the candle flame while stating the conjuring sentence over and over again.

Travel astrally to your sacred place, while repeating the words: Come (name of spirit), come forth and reveal yourself unto me, come and answer my request for thee, and so mote it be, in the name and honour of thee, blessed Lord and Lady.

Repeat these words astrally, while entering your sacred space. Present yourself and the purpose of the conjuration. Tell the entities after the binding words, that they shall go through your spiritual and astral bodies into your physical body, and from there into the vessel that you hold in your physical bodys left hand (or to perfom the charge that you give them).

When you have established the connection and told the charge, state out loud: I bind thee, of light eternally, I bind thee of light eternally!

Repeat this until you have returned to your physical body. Envision how you take the entity in its hand while travelling back. See how your white cord is drawing you back the physical body while holding the entities hand.

While you hold the vessel in your left hand, place the right above it and state out loud (this is a very common binding words for witches today, but I suggest that you after some experience write your own binding words) Sealed and bound you are forever. Bound through the fires of respect and honour. You are intended to the care and companionship of all keepers of this, your vessel. Dicarno sevetek oprenus two see garanox.

The goethic voodoo doll

Theres multitudes of interesting ways of constructing the famed waxdoll of majics.

No way is the right way, other than the one most fitting for your own personal majical system. It takes many experiments on different targets in your close surroundings to polish your ritual performances into a nice diamond to be used at your finest parties so to speak.

Make sure to document every detail in all of your experiments. Study the effects upon your target closely, document the effects and the timing of those effects, along with your technics used.

Waxdolls, and other forms of representative objects have been used for majical purposes in many majical systems and cultures through history. The most famed ones in present time, is probably the voodoo dolls, or the salomonic wax doll.

Most people have heard the story about the mythological creation of the Golem that haunted the citizens of prag a long time ago, created by Rabbi Judah Loew for protection of the jewish population.

This excellent example shows how potent this form of majic is, and how its power grows with time. It also teaches us how important it is with complete control over your majical creation.

In ancient egypt it was very common to produce little clay dolls of enemies, or just clay tablets with the names of enemies along with the written curse. For a long period of time they used to bury these tablets, or dolls on abandoned grave sites, so that the spirits present would carry out the charge of the curse for them.

Traces of this technic can still be found in many majical systems, feks the hoodoo practicioners way of envoyer les morts, sending the dead, when they perform so called expeditions, death spells, upon their enemies with the help of Baron Cimetiere.

In egypt, we called upon Anubis for such charges.

Forms of egregoire practice can be traced all the way to hunter gatherer societies, were the shaman used to enter the underworld through a cave, and make a representative drawing of the tribes wanted prey upon the cave wall and then do their majics to attract the prey towards the tribes hunters.

These drawings often evolved into whole scenes with hunters surrounding the prey throwing spears, or shooting arrows at it.

They imprinted the wanted outcome of the hunt upon the walls in the underworld, and then called upon the spiritual forces to support the wanted outcome of the hunt. The tribes egregoire was sent to carry out their charge for them.

A very effective way of manifesting your desires into the reality of this realm fast.

A few of the ancient technics can be found in the various practices of the craft today.

In ancient days, the highpriest and the highpriestess had a ritual intercourse in front of the coven, and after, the highpriestess went through a symbolized birth of the egregoire spirit through the making of the waxdoll. She symbolized the whole birthprocess of the doll.

After the birth, the doll was given the three breaths of life from the highpriest and then it was ready for majic rite.

The energies produced during the climax of female and male efforts was a very powerful energy to be used in the creation of the egregoire spirit, emphazied by its ritual birth and the precense of divine powers during the whole ritual.

The highpriestess red cord, was tied around her waist in one end, the other to the doll, and after birth, the cord was cut, like in a real birth.

Traces of this practice can still be found in various wicca covens during the seventies and eighties revival of the craft.

If you have a partner, I recomend to use a form of this technic when creating your wax doll. Then you have to make sure that both of you channel all of the energy created during climax into the waxdoll.

I suggest that you perform the act within a conjured circle of power, with the watchtowers, the lord and the lady present. The incense should be Lotus incense, and you should have offerings of one glass of red wine to the lord, and one for the lady. You should also lit three white candles in the name and honour of the lord and the lady, and let them burn during your rite. It is best performed during the yule sabbath, when the birth of the sunking is celebrated, but it could be performed at any fullmoon sabbath.

The waxdoll can be produced for many purposes, not only dark majics as most belives today, but it could also be used as a means to place white majic upon your target, or just to produce a powerful egregoire to work for you or the coven. Just make sure to have its purpose and charge clear before you start the production of it. If you dont give it purpose and a clear charge, it will find its own charges, and those might not be the ones that you wished for, just as in the golem story of ancient Prag.

Speak to, and treat your waxdoll, as you would to the real person, or spirit that you have created. If you dont have a partner, this ritual can be performed with spiritual assistance, with feks a powerful succubus, or a nymph spirit for the gentlemen and a powerful incubus for the the female practicioner.

Many magicians prefer this technic, as the spiritual entities helps to produce more powerful energies for the majics wished for. Here I can recomend to use a powerful demon, or a water nymph, a siren, or a djinn, as they produce very high energy in this technic.

The wax doll

Ingridiendts...

- Holy water and salt from a fullmoon sabbath
- dragons blood incense
- lotus incense
- some fine quality honey
- beeswax, or candlewax from your ritual candle holders as they contains powerful energies from your rites.
- a taglock from your prey, or just a piece of fine quality paper with the written name and birthdate or your prey.
- Melt the wax in an earthen pot, in a conjured circle of power.
- mix into it a few ounches of dragons blood incense, some honey and the taglock of your prey

When the wax is starting to cool down, shape it like youre inteded prey. make a little doll out of it.

Use your athame to carve the name of your prey upon your doll.

Then you evoke apophis, typhoon, sol the destroyer, Isis and Osiris to charge and empower your doll for you.

I recommend to use the seals of the seventh book of moses to empower the doll. Inscribe the seals of the angels of wraith, or the plagues, if you intend to do dark majics.

When you have produced the physical doll, charge it with energy, sending through your right hand.

Envision solar energy and the sun as it looks from space when you empower it.

Hypnotic inductive conjuration

"My friend, did you not call me? Why have I wakened?
Did you not touch me? Why am I startled?
Did a god not pass by? Why is my flesh frozen numb?
My friend, I have had the third dream!"
-Gilgamesh

Introduction

Relaxation

Your body starts to feel more and more heavy. Everything around you becomes dark, empty space. A calm and familiar darkness blankets your senses.

Relax and focus your mind on your feet. Feel how your mind releases them into complete weightlessness, like they are levitating in midair by itself. A warm prickeling sensation spreads through every particle that your feet are made of. It feels nice and soothing.

This feeling slowly spreads up your legs towards the pelvis, stomach and chest.

For every breath you take, the sensation spreads further through your limbs, until you are completely relaxed. Focus on your slow, rhythmic breathing. It fills your body in a harmonic symphony of relaxation. Nothing else matters.

Your body levitates on a warm summer breeze.

Script 1, the cave

As the sun warms up your body, you find yourself sitting in a comfortable chair on a vast beach.

Your feet are buried deep into the cool sand.

Listen to the waves that crashes into the shore in a calm but steady force of nature. Feel the smell of the salty sea, the sea weed and sand.

You are completely relaxed and secure.

As you slowly rise up from the chair and turn around, you see a vast field of grass and colorful flowers in front of you. A large, beautiful butterfly flaps its majestic wings on an everlasting journey to collect the life giving nectar of each flower on the field.

There is a narrow path through the grass towards a large mountain at the end of the field. You feel drawn towards it. There is something familiar and soothing about that mountain. You know this place, and it makes you happy.

The green grass tickles your legs as you start walking towards the mountain.

As you come closer, and closer, and closer, you see a large dark cave opening up in front of you. There is a large fierce red dragon sitting next to the opening. He is the guardian of the cave and its treasures.

The dragon turns around and looks deep into your eyes for a moment. He knows you, and you are welcome here. You belong here, you are completely relaxed and secure. Nothing can hurt you.

As you step into the cave, you feel the cold stone under your bare feet. You stop for a moment to look around you. It's a large chamber full of dripping stalaktites and small ponds of water that slowly grows under them. The mesmerizing dripping sounds echoes through every corner of the chamber.

Moist, cool air fills your lungs with every breath, as you start walking towards a tunnel at the edge of the chamber.

There is a pair of torches burning by the entrance to the tunnel. You know this tunnel very well, and you also know that there are twelve pairs of torches following the tunnel towards the main hall.

As you start walking through the dark tunnel, you silently count down for each set of torches that you pass on your way towards the main hall.

Twelve, is the number of the great work, your opus magnum. You feel completely relaxed.

Eleven, is strength and fortitude. Your body and mind are one.

Ten, is your fate. You feel happy and excited to be were you belong. Nothing can harm you here.

Nine, the soothing smell of burning torches lead your way towards wisdom and insight. You will remember.

Eight, is balance and authority. You feel more and more secure as you pass each set of torches. You are completely relaxed.

Seven, is the number of your journey through this sacred mountain. You walk deeper and deeper into the dark tunnel.

Six, is unity and love. The comforting symphony of dripping water echoes between the tunnel walls as you keep counting the torches.

Five, is your key. There is a pentacle on the wall. In the distance, you can see the final set of torches.

Four, you rule over your own destiny with respect and honour.

Three, this is the beginning and the end of all things. You walk on the border of time and space. Here you decide when and where you want to go.

Two, the smell of flowers calm your senses as you walk deeper and deeper into the hidden caverns of mother earth.

One, the final set of flaming torches lit up the familiar entrance to the main hall. Its light shows the way into the most secret and sacred of places. There is a marble pillar on each side of the entrance, one is black and the other is white. The two passwords into the hall is inscribed upon the pillars and you read them out loud. –Jakin! Boas! The text starts to glow in a vibrant purple fiery haze.

Script 2, the main hall

A dimly lit pathway spread the darkness of the main hall. At its end a large balefire starts to burn. The flames seem to dance with the gust of howling winds as it reaches towards the unseen walls of the cavern.

You walk down the path and up to the balefire. As you stand there and look into the glowing pieces of oak wood in the firepit, you start to feel an overwhelming precense that obsersves you from the darkness behind you, silently waiting.

It is time to do what you have come for, so you sit down on your knees in front of the sparkling fire. The heat spreads upon your skin while you think of the name and seal of the lord of the forest. The mountain king and magician.

You feel relaxed and completely safe. You look forward to his mighty precense.

When you feel ready, you start to draw his name and seal, with fiery energy upon the ground in front of you. First you draw the circle with horns, and then the "K".

As you cross the arms upon your chest in deep respect, you start calling his name. –Kernunnos, Osiris, Apollo, Pan half beast, half man. I summon and conjure thee, in the name and honour of the Lord and the Lady. Come, I pray! Come, I say!

His powerful precense fills the dense air around you as you see a large shadow moving around in the darkness. It is darker than the darkest of darkness itself.

The shadow slowly moves towards the edge of the illuminating fire with heavy footsteps, until it starts to form a towering sillouette in the distance. You can see the shape of his majestic deer antlers, his muscular body and goat legs, as you feel an intense burst of fiery, male energy surge through your limbs.

He welcomes you with a comforting nood, and awaits your words.

The heavy smell of musk and pine forest fills your nostrils as you greet him, and thank him for coming to your call.

Take a moment to speak with him as you would to a close friend. Relax and enjoy the moment. You are completely safe.

Script 3, past lifes

When you feel ready, you ask the magician if he can help you to see past lifes.

He looks at you while he slowly raises his right hand and points towards a tunnel of light behind him.

You thank him, and start walking towards the light in the distance. You feel completely relaxed, and secure. You will remember everything you feel, smell, hear and see.

The warm light is brighter at the end of the tunnel and you are drawn towards it. Completely weightless, levitating peacefully.

You enter the light and float in the air. As you enjoy the blissfull and happy feeling of the warm light, you hear birds singing around you.

You find yourself hanging in the air above a large field of summer green grass covered with beautiful flowers in all colors. A large butterfly majesticly flaps its wings on an everlasting journey of collecting the life giving nectar of each and every flower. Relax, and remember.

A tunnel of bright light is forming behind the butterfly and you are drawn towards it. You know that at the end of the tunnel, you will experience and remember a past incarnation that is important for you and your great work.

At first everything is just bright white light all around you. Relax, nothing can hurt you here.

You can feel how you enter the body at the moment of its death. Time slowly rewinds, and you carefully remember everything you feel, smell, hear and see.

Take a moment to stop and experience what you see.

Look around you. What do you see?

Explore every sense in this time and space.

Listen! What do you hear?

Breath! What do you smell?

Feel! How does it feel?

Think! What are your happy moments? What kind of problems concerns you?

Nothing can hurt you here. You are completely relaxed and secure.

Script 4, past lifes, coming back

In the distance you can see a field of flowers in all colors. You notice a large butterfly that majesticly flaps its wings on an everlasting journey to collect the lifegiving nectar of each and every flower. Behind it a tunnel vortex of vibrant white light is opening up. You feel drawn into it.

You are completely relaxed as you peacefully levitate through the tunnel of light on a warm summer breeze.

As you enter the light at the end of the tunnel you feel the suns warm rays spread across your face and body. And you find yourself floating in the air high above a field of flowers.

Script 5, in between lifes

After a moment, you start to see and feel the presence of other beings around you. You feel welcomed and at home again. So you land on the field under you, next to a crystal clear lake. Everything goes in slow motion, time and space is nonexistent here.

As you land with one foot at a time, you feel the dewy grass tickle your legs in a loving embrace.

You know this place. It is where you are in between incarnations, between lifes.

Take a moment to explore your surroundings, and remember.

What do you hear, smell, see and feel. Remember.

When you feel ready, you sit down next to the crystal clear lake. Here you can see your true self in the reflection of the lake. Some are afraid of the monsters hidden under the surface. But you are not that, you embrace them all with love and understanding.

An exhilarating feeling of divine bliss and harmony fills your empty body as you understand yourself and what you are.

There is a swan feather floating over the reflection of you. A beautiful strong swan must have placed it there for you. When you pick it up, you feel a rush of warm energy fill your body. It is the feather of wisdom, and with it, you will always remember this place and your true self.

When you seek answers, you will just think of this feather and you will know.

Script 6, in between lifes, back to the cave

You start to notice the dripping sound from the cave halls somewhere behind you. And you feel drawn towards its mesmerizing calming drips into calm pools of water. So you start walking towards the sound.

A tunnel of light appears before you, and you swiftly float through it towards the dark main hall, the cave. You stop in front of the towering dark precense of the magician, the lord of the forest.

You smile at him, and thank him for guiding you so lovingly. You proudly show him the soft white feather in your hand before you start walking towards the long cave with the 12 torches.

When you wake up you will think of the swan feather and remember everything.

You start counting each set of flaming torches of the wall.

1. you slowly come back to yourself again.
2. you feel completely safe, nothing can harm you, and you will remember.
3. with every step you take, with every set of torches that you pass by, you feel the mind and body as one.
4. you become aware of the limbs of your body, more and more for each torch that you pass.

5. when you come to the last set, you will be completely awake, and remember. You will still hold on to the soft white swan feather. It will be with you forever.

6. focus on your breathing, how you inhale and exhale. With each life giving breath that you take, you will more, and more awake.

7. now you continue counting the torches until you reach the last one, nr 12. Then you will stretch out your body and feel completely awake again.